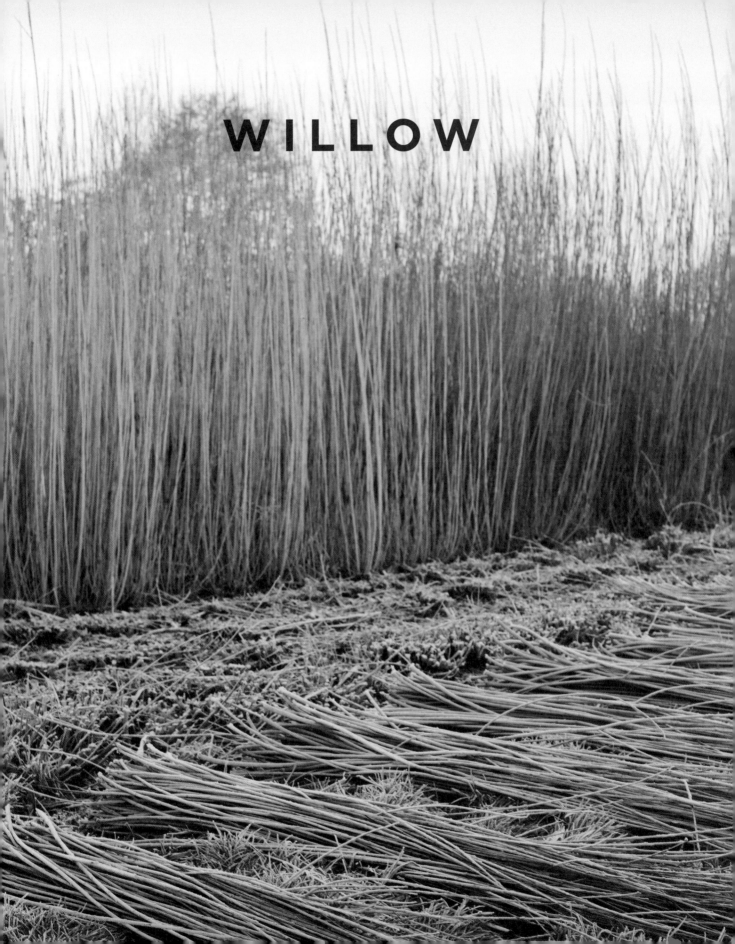

WILLOW

WILLOW

A GUIDE TO GROWING AND HARVESTING
PLUS 20 BEAUTIFUL WOVEN PROJECTS

JENNY CRISP

PHOTOGRAPHY BY SARAH WEAL

jacqui
small

First published in 2018
A Jacqui Small book for White Lion Publishing,
part of the Quarto Group
1 Triptych Place, 2nd Floor,
London, SE1 9SH, United Kingdom
T (0)20 7700 6700 F (0)20 7700 8066
www.Quarto.com

Publisher: Jacqui Small
Design and Art Direction: Rachel Cross
Editor: Sian Parkhouse
Photographer: Sarah Weal
Stylist: Caroline Davis
Production: Maeve Healy

The author has made every attempt to draw attention to safety
precautions, but it is the reader's responsibility to ensure safety
practices while carrying out techniques outlined in this book.

ISBN: 978-1-911127-71-0

A catalogue record for this book is available from
the British Library.

2024
10 9

Printed in China

A note on measurements:
Dimensions and measurements are given in
metric and Imperial. Please follow one system
consistently, and do not combine the two.

CONTENTS

WILLOW: ANCIENT AND MODERN

Basket making is one of the oldest crafts known to man. Currently, we can date some found pieces as far back as Mesolithic times. For thousands of years, every community across the world has woven their indigenous materials into dwellings, means of transportation, functional objects for use in the home and garden and even into clothing and jewellery. Grasses were woven into shoes, cloaks or carpets, while branches of small trees were woven into boxes, boats or houses. The knowledge and understanding of these materials would have created an unquestionable symbiosis with nature and the environment. Survival depended on this deep-rooted knowledge.

Very little changed until the 20th century. In most communities, rural and urban, there would have been an area of land close by that was used to grow willow. Really, it wasn't until the 1960s, with the explosion of man-made materials and cheap international transportation, that the growing of willow and the basket making industry came under threat. The links between growing, harvesting and making with willow would until then have been common to many people, but it took only one generation for us to lose these connections. This way of life was no longer familiar or instinctive; we had become separate from it.

Today, little has changed in the processes of cultivating and manufacturing objects in willow. Unlike other crafts, such as weaving fabric, potting, woodworking and blacksmithing, basket making has escaped the developments of the industrial revolution.

There are many types of willow suitable for basket making and they grow into as many different dimensions, densities, colours and textures. They each have their own particular quality, which, in turn, dictates how they are used. We haven't yet been able to invent a machine that can make a basket, because we cannot standardize what mother nature produces. Fortunately, we cannot force willow to grow into a uniform material that works with the precise needs of mechanization. For this reason, willow weaving is a craft that resists the forces and developments of modern life. The tools and workshops in the basket-making world today have changed little over time – if we could walk into a basket maker's workshop in 16th-century London, we would find very little difference in the method of production from the processes I use in my workshop today.

In the 21st century we are trying to reconnect with nature by choice, and not by necessity. We have moved from wanting to keep nature out of our daily lives to seeking to include it. Our mechanized and digital lives have become so separated from our surroundings that some people seek a personal dialogue with nature and their environment in one way or another. Many of us aspire to question and to re-engage with a knowledge and understanding of our materials, with the hope that we can tap into an ancient and cultural memory that once existed. A hero of mine, the environmental sculptor Andy Goldsworthy, stands as a testament to this. He gathers and reorders nature, with very few tools, to create breathtaking natural compositions that he hopes reminds us of this lost connection.

A variety of basket-making willows, cut in January, sorted and drying naturally in the sunshine (opposite).

WORKING WITH WILLOW

THERE ARE MANY, MANY DIFFERENT WAYS OF WEAVING
A BASKET WITH WILLOW. WORLDWIDE THERE ARE AS
MANY VARIATIONS OF TECHNIQUES AS THERE ARE TYPES OF
WILLOW. OVER THE CENTURIES DIFFERENT CULTURES HAVE
BEEN INCREDIBLY INGENIOUS IN THE WAYS IN WHICH THEY
HAVE INTERPRETED THIS REMARKABLE MATERIAL
TO MAKE THEIR BASKETS.

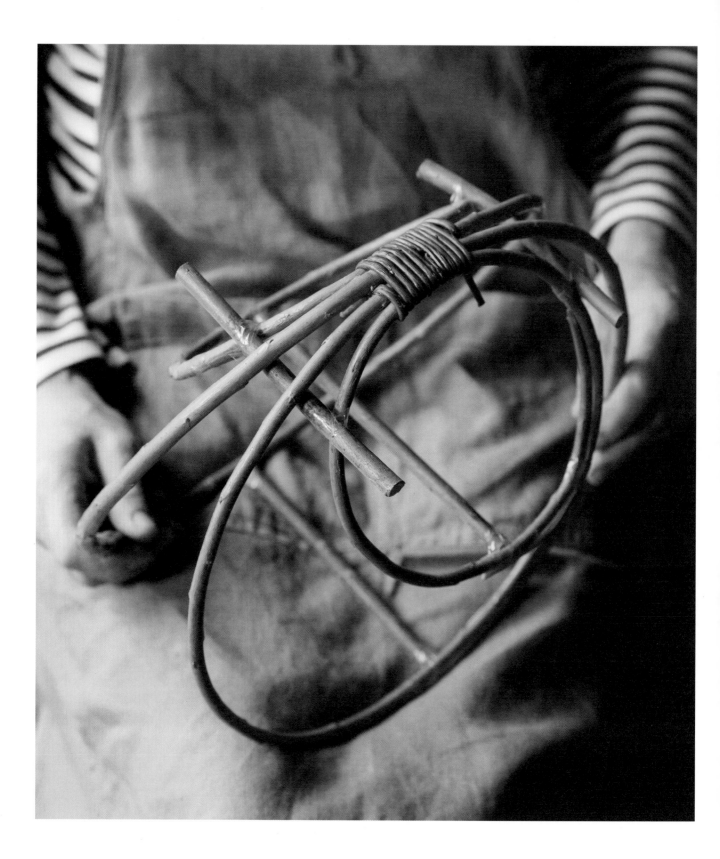

WHY I WORK WITH WILLOW

I have been a professional willow grower and basket maker for more than 30 years. I have set out to earn a living making functional baskets from homegrown materials, and to practise using the inherent nature of those materials to the best of my knowledge, ability and experience. My aim is to be innovative while retaining a respect for the old patterns and traditions of this craft.

In 1985 I completed a BA (Hons) in woven textiles at West Surrey College of Art and Design and I left qualified to weave fabric for upholstery. For my thesis I decided I would research the use of willow for basket making, thinking I might combine this with the practical side of the course. During the research I came across a couple who, unbeknown to me, would have a fundamental impact on my career choice and way of life.

Judy and David Drew lived in a beautiful Somerset cob house that they had sympathetically renovated. They lived about as far from digital and industrial development as was possible in 20th-century Britain. They were almost self-sufficient in food and willow. David was a full-time willow grower and basket maker, with an expert knowledge and understanding of his environment and all that it could provide. I was hooked. Growing up with practical parents, a love of the outdoors and a lot of energy, I had found the life for me. Sponsored by the Crafts Council, I was fortunate to spend one year apprenticed to David. We worked together on and off for the following five years.

So, for three decades now I have grown willow and made baskets. I have been lucky enough to work with the seasons and out in the elements, growing a material that keeps me connected to nature and my environment. To master the use of willow you must first understand its characteristics and qualities. A perfect basket depends on the maker's empathy with the material and tools, on repetition and experience, combined with the intention in the maker's mind. This practice requires slow and steady observation; repetition allows for mindful development in understanding the material. My working life gives me a questioning, rudimentary symbiosis with nature and the environment, and I will always feel privileged to be in this position.

Many years ago it was common for a basket maker to serve an apprenticeship lasting anywhere between three and five years. This meant that he or she would have enough experience and knowledge of materials, tools and products to be able to perform the craft to a high standard with speed and efficiency in order to make strong baskets and to earn a living. Sadly, today it's unusual to find opportunities for apprenticeships. This knowledge is still valued, but it is hard to find other than through books or weekend courses.

I hope the information and advice included in this book, along with the range of projects chosen, will enable you to share the essence of making an object from a natural material, and that you will have the opportunity to experience the delightful fulfilment that growing willow and basket making can bring.

The start of a gathering basket, using sticks to space the templates ready for weaving (opposite).

GROWING FOR MAKING

Growing willow to make things is a rewarding process, with relatively quick results. If you have an area in your garden around the size of a double garage you have enough room to grow a few different species of willow. Within 12 months of planting you will be able to use some of your own material to make some of the projects in this book.

Willow, sometimes called sallow or osier, or by its botanical name of *Salix*, grows as deciduous trees or shrubs. They are found primarily on moist soil in cold and temperate regions in the northern hemisphere. Willow has many qualities that make it suited to the manufacturing of baskets over and above other woods such as ash, chestnut, hazel or oak. Traditionally, these types of woods were pollarded approximately every seven years. Pollarding, or coppicing, is a system of pruning strong growth close to the trunk to promote a dense head of straight and usable material. Willow seems to thrive when pruned annually, and this one-year growth gives an abundance of supple material suitable for weaving. There are around 400 species, each with its own inherent character. Not all willows work well for basket making, and so over the centuries certain species have been cultivated to produce good working material to suit the maker and item needed. This one-year growth is very pliable and grows very long, and the stools from which it is cut recover quickly to provide a healthy, sustainable, crop suitable for weaving for many years.

UNDERSTANDING WILLOW

Every year, nature provides the basket maker with a broad palette of subtle colour and patina, but willow has other, more important, qualities the maker needs to be aware of. Different varieties differ greatly in the way they grow, and in the dimension and density of the wood. For example, the species *Salix viminalis* can grow up to 4m (14ft) in one year. The diameter of the thick butt end of these rods can be anything up to 3cm (1in) wide, making them useful for large outdoor structures. To achieve this phenomenal growth rate this vigorous willow needs to draw enormous amounts of water and minerals from the ground, giving the rods a large ratio of pith to wood, sometimes making them a soft willow. *S. purpurea* is a slender, elegant willow with a beautiful glossy patina, but it only grows up to 2.2m (7ft) in one year. This slower growth gives a smaller pith-to-wood ratio, and so the wood is harder. This makes an excellent, hard-wearing species for long-lasting, elegant baskets.

The species *S. triandra*, *S. daphnoides* and *S. alba* are also commonly grown for making baskets. Within each of these, there are many varieties and hybrids with curious names such as 'Dicky Meadows', 'Nancy Saunders', 'Slender Tip' and 'Petite Grisette'. For those of you who would like to try your hand at growing a little of your own material, my advice would be to begin with only four to five different types of basket making willow with varying growth rates, which will give you some choice in scale and density. Having a smaller choice of material at the outset means you will get to know your willows and how to use them more quickly. To start you off, buy cuttings from a specialist supplier of basket-making willow.

Gathering freshly cut, unsorted willow on a beautiful winter's day (opposite).

CHOOSING YOUR SITE

Willow grows naturally in open spaces, along riverbanks and pond shores, in a wide range of soils. Fertile, lowland sites with deep, well-drained soils that have a high water table are most suitable.

The small-scale grower may not have access to these ideal conditions, but as long as the site chosen somewhat replicates the natural conditions of willow, very good results can be achieved. Most open, low-lying sites with deep, stone-free soil will provide a productive willow bed. My own bed lies 50cm (1½ft) below sea level, so has a high water table, and it is a very open site that runs alongside a railway line (see the photograph above). Shallow, very alkaline soils, acid peat-based soils or badly drained stagnant conditions are not suitable. Poor soils produce a poor crop that will also be prone to pests and disease. Do not plant near any pipework.

A willow bed is quick to establish and cultivation is simple. Clear the ground of weeds and turn the soil: this allows the roots to grow freely. After soil preparation, you need to make a decision in relation to weed control. This is essential in the first year particularly, to allow the cuttings to develop into strong, healthy plants. Hand-weeding, planting through a breathable membrane or laying down a thick mulch, such as bark, are all options.

Square beds give straighter, slender rods and better results than long, thin beds, as willow grown on the outsides of the beds tends to be bushier and less straight, as it has more light and less competition. It's also important to avoid stool competition. Large, fast-growing varieties will out-compete slower-growing ones, so in a mixed bed it's best put the taller, more vigorous varieties on the north side and the smaller, finer varieties on the south side, to avoid one being in the shade of the other.

PLANTING YOUR WILLOW BED

Planting takes place during the dormant winter months, any time between November and March. Any later in the spring and you run the risk of drought damage. Insert root-free, fresh (green) cuttings into tilled, weed-free ground. Cuttings are mostly taken from one- or two-year-old plants, from which you can take four to five cuttings starting at the thick (butt) end. A cutting is usually around 30cm (1ft) long.

Your rows need to be at least 60cm (24in) apart, (80cm/32in for larger varieties), and the settings, or sets, 30cm (12in) apart in the row (60cm/24in for larger varieties). This dense way of planting ensures that new shoots have to compete for light and so grow long, straight and clean of branches. It also restricts weed growth. Push at least half the length of the cutting into the ground to ensure good root growth. Be careful to plant the cuttings the right way up – the buds need to be pointing upwards – otherwise they will die. Controlling weed growth is essential for good-quality material. In the first season, some watering will be necessary in dry periods, because at this stage the roots will be very fine and close to the surface, so will dry out more easily.

No other trees can compete with the growth rate of willow. They can completely screen an area within nine months of planting. By late autumn the annual growing cycle for a basket willow is complete. This is when the sap has stopped flowing and the leaf has fallen. Your willows are now fully grown and ready to harvest. This willow bed will give a healthy crop for up to 20 years.

Trench digging to secure a weed-suppressing membrane (below left). Planting willow cuttings (below right).

HARVESTING WILLOW

Harvesting your own material to make into a basket is a very rewarding process, and it starts with cutting your crop during the dormant period. Willows are dormant between November and February, and will supply at that time a year's growth of very long and flexible material suitable to weave with. When cut at this point, willow is know as 'green' (see page 19).

In the first year, depending on variety, you will have four to eight shoots of varying lengths on one stool. As the years go by, the number of shoots cut from these stools will increase, doubling and then tripling your harvest. After three years your stools of willow achieve maximum production and will sustain this for ten years or more.

CUTTING

Willows can be cut by hand or by machine. The stools from which the rods grow are cut close to the ground, leaving a stump that will shoot as the sap rises again in spring, to provide next year's harvest. Commercial growers use specialist machinery that magically cuts and bundles at great speed. For the smaller grower, such as myself, a strimmer with a 60-tooth blade and a very steady hand is adequate. However, the very first crop of willows you cut from your bed really needs to be cut by hand. The stools have not yet developed a strong enough root system, and are not yet anchored enough to withstand the rather more vigorous process of machine cutting. Cutting by hand with a good pair of secateurs or a sharp knife is perfectly feasible for the smaller grower – it is actually my preferred way of harvesting, but sadly it is too slow for the scale on which I grow.

SORTING

After cutting, fresh willow rods need to be sorted and bundled. It's important to keep different varieties separate so that you can become familiar with the varying qualities they have to offer. As previously mentioned, different species of willow will grow to different lengths in one year. However, the growth rate within each species also varies, and so this mixed growth needs to be graded into bundles of assorted lengths. Trying to make an object with unsorted willow is like trying to weave with human-sized spaghetti.

Cutting willow by hand with a knife (left).
Freshly cut willow graded to length in the foreground, with unsorted willow in the background (opposite).

To grade these assorted lengths you will need to fix a long upright pole, marked every 30cm (1ft), to the side of a large container such as a rubbish bin (trash can) or barrel. Drop a handful of unsorted willow firmly into the container so that all the cut ends drop to the base. Then, from the top of the bundle, pull out all the rods whose tips stand between the top two marks on your pole. So, for example, from a bundle of ungraded 'Dicky Meadows' you can pull out the longest rods that measure anywhere between 180 and 220cm (6 and 7ft).

Next, after re-dropping the remaining rods back into the barrel (again, done with some force to ensure that all the butts connect with the base of the container),

pull out the rods that measure between 150 and 180cm (5 and 6ft). Continue like this until you are down to lengths of less than 30 cm (1ft). For me, anything less than this is too small to use.

During this process reject rough or branched rods unsuitable for making. As you work your way through the mixed pile of rods your sorted piles grow, giving you beautifully graded materials, so that when you come to select for making your choice is far easier to judge.

DRYING AND STORING

Freshly cut and sorted bundles of willow need to dry out thoroughly before they can be stored indoors. Rather like the process of seasoning wood, this allows the material to steadily dry out without going mouldy. It will reach a stable state, ready to store for use in the future. Depending on length, thickness and drying conditions, this can take anything from 8 to 20 weeks. In all storage stages the bundles need to be kept off the ground so that the air can circulate around the cut ends – this ensures that they don't root again or go rotten.

Immediately after cutting, willow can be stored outside for a while. After a few weeks you will notice that the bark on the rods shows signs of shrinkage. The rods are now half dry and need to be put under cover, sheltered from the rain but not enclosed completely, as they will start to compost without air circulation. At this stage it is possible to bend the rods to a right angle without cracking. In this 'semi-green' state (see opposite), you could make a basket with your harvested willow, without the need to dry, store and re-soak (see page 22).

Once completely dry your willow can be stored in a shed, garage or spare bedroom until needed. In this state, it's no longer possible to bend the rods to a right angle without cracking. Thoroughly dry bundles of willow stored in an airy room can last for years.

WILLOW CATEGORIES

Should the idea of growing your own material not appeal you can buy willow directly from the grower (see page 144). This willow comes in four different conditions. These descriptions, while vaguely referring to the colour, more precisely refer to the physical condition of the rods.

Brown willow

This term refers to all varieties of willow that still have the bark on. The colours can be any of nature's innate colours. They range from deep red and yellow to chestnut, purple and rich mahogany. Different patinas give texture as well as colour to play with. It has been cut, dried and is ready to be soaked, and is available all year round.

Green willow

This is recently cut willow. In this condition it is mostly sold as cuttings for planting, or used for building outdoor, living structures such as sculpture or fencing. It can be easily worked for basket making, but will shrink a lot, resulting in a loosely woven object. However, half-dry or semi-green willow can be used in places, and will retain a more vibrant colour. It is available November to March.

White (stripped) willow

Willow with the bark stripped off is an altogether different material, considered more refined. Beneath the bark all willows are white, but only certain varieties respond to this process. It is available in late spring or early summer.

Buff willow

Willow that has been boiled with its bark on and then stripped is known as 'buff'. The tannins in the bark dye the wood underneath to the colour of a strong cup of tea. Willow in this condition is available all year round.

PREPARING FOR WEAVING

Prior to weaving, any willow used for basket making has to be soaked. For the projects in this book I use brown willow. You might prefer to buy your material, so I cover the different preparation for all types of willow. For the newcomer, there will be a certain amount of trial and error in understanding these processes, but it's worth taking your time with this, as working with perfectly soaked and mellowed material is a dream.

SOAKING

Green or semi-green
Willow in this condition cannot be soaked at all. These rods, even though they are cut when dormant, still retain some sap, which resists water.

White and buff
Without bark, these rods absorb water much more quickly, in a matter of hours. The advantage of this is that your preparation time is much more flexible. You can decide what you would like make and be ready to start weaving an hour or two later. Again, soaking times vary according to the thickness of your rods, but only by minutes.

Brown
These willows take the longest to soak, sometimes up to ten days, so some forward planning is necessary. On the whole, the theory of soaking one day for every 30cm (1ft) is a helpful guide. However, this will depend on the variety of willow you use (because the density of wood varies), the season and the climate. For example, a 180cm (6ft) bundle of *Salix triandra* 'Black Maul' should take six days, but this can vary by two days either way.

Here are a few helpful guidelines to how to take care of your brown willow when it's out of the tank (see page 27), and how to enhance its flexibility before making.

Allow the excess water to drain away. Find a place out of the wind and sun and lean your bundles against a wall for an hour or two. You will notice a change of colour but, more importantly, the very structure of the wood changes, too. It seems to transform into a different composition. To test if your willow has reached this state, and is ready or not, simply bend one rod gently to a right angle. If the bark doesn't crack on the back, your willow is ready to use.

If it is under-soaked, the bark or possibly even the wood will crack. If it does, return your bundle to the water for another day and test again. If it is over-soaked, it will feel slimy and the bark will be loose or even fall off when rubbed. It's hard to recover over-soaked willow. It's worth trying to mellow it for a few hours (see below), but if that doesn't work it's best to start again, as working with over-soaked material is not a pleasant experience.

MELLOWING
When you are satisfied that all the willow is soaked adequately, prepare a wet cloth and piece of plastic large enough to wrap all of the willow you have soaked. Then, having allowed the excess water to drain, wrap it in

As a professional basket maker, I regularly soak a tank full of willow, which will keep me busy for two or three weeks. In this batch I include different varieties of rods in varying lengths, according to what I intend to make (opposite).

the cloth and then the plastic. White and buff willow needs to be wrapped minutes after draining; brown, as mentioned, is left longer before mellowing.

MAINTAINING FLEXIBILITY

When I am teaching I regularly come across much confusion about how to maintain willow in good working condition over periods of time. The most important thing to consider is that your material, once soaked and mellowed, will constantly change its pliability according to the circumstances of the space you are working in. For example, a dry and sunny room means your material will become brittle more quickly than if you are working in a cellar with a cool, even temperature. If you want to work outdoors (which is impossible with white and buff willow), a breezy, sunny day will dry out brown willow quicker than a damp overcast day. It's important for you as a maker to tune into these changes, to be able to manage your material well.

Building a basket in brown willow is more leisurely than in white or buff, because the bark holds the moisture in the rod for longer and, if handled carefully, it can stay workable for two to three weeks. To achieve this, the balance of air and moisture needs to be understood. If you were to keep your brown bundles continuously wrapped during this period, after three to four days they would start to break down and compost, so it's important to unwrap them each day to allow the air to circulate. Remember to wrap them in a damp cloth and plastic at night to retain enough moisture to keep them workable for use the following day.

When building a basket in white or buff willow you need to be able to complete your piece quickly without interruptions, as it dries so quickly. Many makers spray the basket regularly with water as it is being made to keep the material workable or, if possible, you can place the whole piece back into the tank for a short time. At the end of the working day, white and buff willow should be stood up and allowed to dry thoroughly, then re-soaked the next day if needed. If you were to keep this willow wrapped overnight and then for hours the next day it would become slimy and unpleasant to use, so it's best to prepare only what you need for the project in mind.

SORTING SOAKED MATERIAL

A basket is rarely made from rods of all the same length or thickness. Each length and thickness has its particular place in the object to be woven, and this varies according to the item being made. Usually there will be at least three different sizes of willow used, so even though your bundles of soaked material have been graded into 30cm (1ft) lengths, within these bundles you will notice that the thickness of the rods varies. It's important to separate them into at least three groups – of fat, medium and thin – before you start. I consider this to be so important that at the beginning of every course I teach I ask everyone to sit and sort a bundle into these three categories. With practice you will become quicker and more accurate. Sitting on a low workshop chair I begin by picking up a handful of rods, first selecting all the fat ones and putting them to one side, then all the thin ones and putting them to the other side, so I am left with only medium ones in my hand. At the end of the process I'm left with three separate piles of distinct thicknesses. This can be done prior to or after soaking.

A bundle of willow sorted into thin, medium and fat, from left to right. Sorting is a process I enjoy very much – it helps with fluency and speed, quietens the mind and focuses the eye, to allow full concentration on the object to be made (opposite).

WORK SPACE AND TOOLS

Creating a work space to make the projects in this book is relatively straightforward. If you simply want to weave in your spare time, you need a large, uncluttered space with little obstruction, as its very easy to flick forgotten objects from their place while concentrating on very long, rapidly moving rods. Unfortunately, centrally heated houses do not provide the best working conditions as the willow will dry out to a brittle and unworkable state. Since willow is worked damp, a water-resistant floor or a large sheet of plastic is essential.

Humidity is important: even today there are areas in France where basket makers still work in natural caves, as the high humidity and constant temperature provide optimal working conditions. However, I guess not all of us have access to a cave, so a cool, still, unheated room is best. The added benefit is that your home will be filled with the distinctive scent of willow, giving a characteristically earthy smell. Visitors to my house always comment on the wonderful aroma of willow that lingers constantly.

A lot of basket makers used to be gypsies or travelling craftsmen, and so they simply worked outdoors. Dry, sunny, windy days are not especially good, unless you are working with brown willow – buff and white willow will dry out too quickly with even the gentlest of breeze. So if you want to work outside, a windless, overcast day is best.

SEAT AND TABLE

A basket maker's bench and chair are not always necessary, but can be helpful to some of the making processes. Traditionally, makers sat close to the floor on a raised piece of wood called a plank, with the work resting on another plank on their lap, called a 'lap board'. The lap board rested level with the ground, giving the secure surface necessary to build a solid basket. This could be raised up and down on the knees, helping to monitor the angles of the overall form. It's important to find a comfortable position to avoid backache when you work for long periods of time.

I prefer to work on a low chair and at a sloping table on four legs. In my opinion this way of working is more comfortable than the traditional way, and more practical than sitting at a chair and table of ordinary height. If you are low to the ground, your tools and your sorted materials stay neat, tidy and within reach. Working with willow means you are working with a material that resembles oversized spaghetti, which can be awkward to keep organized at ordinary table height. Your working surface needs to have holes drilled into it so you can pin and weight various-sized baskets to it with a bodkin.

HAND TOOLS

A willow worker's tools are few, and have changed little over the centuries. Baskets have been excavated that date as far back as Mesolithic times and looking at their construction confirms that there were some very skilled makers using very sharp tools. It's possible to buy a complete set of tools from large commercial willow growers. Sometimes you can find lovely old ones, with very good steel, in antiques or secondhand shops. For knives and bodkins, Opinel or Vergez Blanchard are good makes, and Felco secateurs can't be beaten.

Using this type of heavy, sturdy bench and low chair is my preferred way of working (opposite).

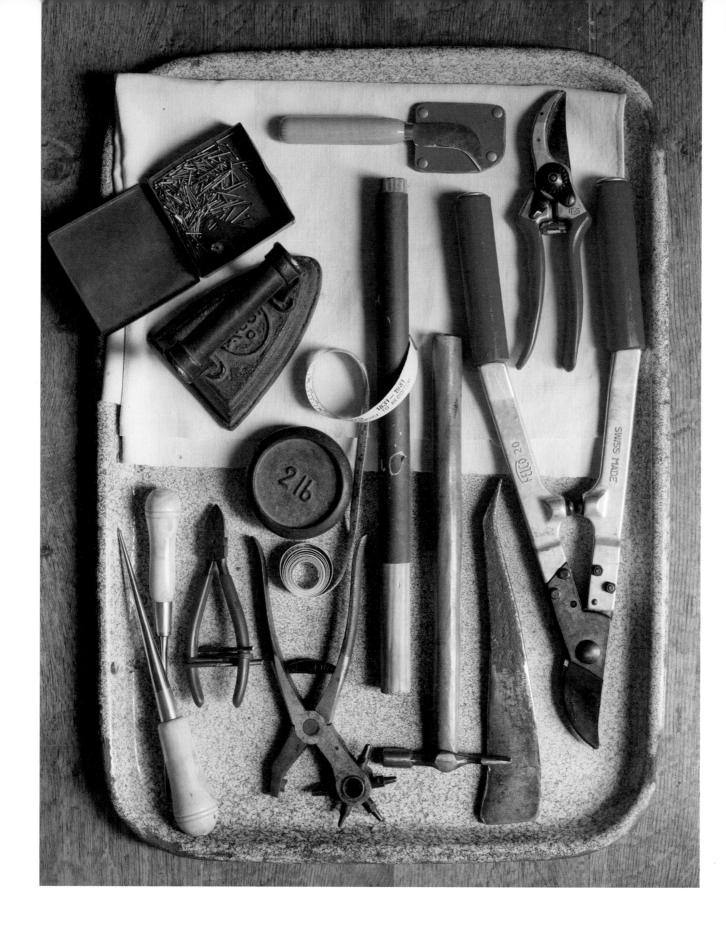

The range of simple tools you will need for the projects in this book:

• **Knife** Used for making many different types of cuts and joins, a basket maker's knife soon becomes a treasured possession. The key to this most favoured tool is for it to feel comfortable in the hand, not too large or heavy, and that it is made of good steel that responds well to regular sharpening. A curved or hooked shape is helpful but not essential.

• **Secateurs** A good pair of secateurs are as important as the knife. Used for preparing and trimming rods, they also need to feel comfortable in the hand and to sharpen well. You may need different sizes if you are working with different sizes of material.

• **Japanese side cutters** This tool performs the same job as the secateurs and looks rather like a pair of pliers. Side cutters are shorter than secateurs, which means you can get into much tighter spaces. The blades are also short and extremely sharp, making it easy to cut very fine pieces of willow.

• **Sharpening tool** Used with a curved knife. To make one wrap very fine wet or dry sandpaper around a piece of broom handle and attach it with double-sided tape.

• **Bodkin** A large, thick, blunt needle-shaped tool, this is used for making spaces between rods in order to insert another rod. It is traditionally used in many different crafts, such as rope making. It's useful to have two sizes to use with varying sizes of work. I also use my thinner bodkin to peg the basket onto the lap board, to make it secure to work on – this allows me to rotate the basket during the build.

• **Hammer and pins** A little tin of panel pins of varying lengths is useful to have, along with a pin hammer.

A complete set of basket-making tools (opposite).

• **Rapping iron/beater** A slim, weighted piece of metal used to beat down your weaving. It can be used heavily to create a very dense weave, or lightly for a lighter weave. For example, a log basket has to work hard in its lifetime and so needs to be beaten well to make it strong, stable and durable. Unbeaten work tends to be loose and flimsy with no structure, and so is short-lived.

• **Weights** These are important when working at a lap board to weigh down work that is pegged to the board with the bodkin. The weight stops the basket from rising up the bodkin and out of position, and helps give you a more solid working position.

• **Measure** A rigid ruler or soft fabric tape will work; regular measuring of diameters and heights is necessary throughout the build.

• **Leather hole punch** A fairly heavy-duty hole punch with a choice of hole sizes is needed to make holes in leather handles so you can attach them.

• **Soaking tank** Used to completely submerge bundles of willow to soak for varying periods of time, this is probably the most expensive item you will need to purchase. A galvanized tank is best. To accommodate long lengths of willow a tank 2m (6½ft) long is useful, with a depth and width of at least 50cm (1½ft). This type of tank is used for watering horses, cattle or sheep, so can be purchased from any farm supply shop. If space or finance is a problem, then it is possible to rig up a temporary tank by draping very thick builder's plastic over a manger of loose bricks. Locating your tank in a shaded area reduces the need to change the water. If you buy a tank with a lip at the top of the rim then you can use this to wedge in your willow with wooden pegs, as it needs to be kept completely submerged during soaking. If you have no rim on your tank very heavy weights, such as bricks, will also work to keep the willow under the water.

KEY TECHNIQUES

THIS SECTION COVERS SOME ESSENTIAL ADVICE ON HOW TO UNDERSTAND THE FUNDAMENTAL QUALITIES OF WILLOW AND HOW TO USE THEM TO YOUR ADVANTAGE. IT INCLUDES INSTRUCTIONS ON HOW TO MAKE THREE BASIC TEMPLATES AND HOW TO COMPLETE FOUR BASIC TECHNIQUES THAT ARE COMMON TO MANY OF THE PROJECTS IN THIS BOOK.

GETTING STARTED

HANDLING WILLOW

Picking up your first willow rod to make a basket is rather daunting. Where do you start? How do you fix separate elements together to make an object? It begins with understanding that in a willow rod, one year's growth will always be thicker at the base end than at the top. You are not working with a continuous, even length of material, as you would with yarn, so every technique, pattern and form is created with this in mind. We use the word butt to describe the thick end and tip to describe the thin end.

Secondly, if you look closely you will notice that every rod grows with a natural curve, which can be used to your advantage at times. This curve varies according to variety, and where it is grown in the willow bed. If you grow your own material you will notice that the rods in the centre of your willow bed will be straighter than those on the outside. We call the inside of the curve the belly and the outside of the curve the back.

Unlike yarn, weaving with willow is somewhat final. If a newly woven basket is taken apart every rod will hold the shape woven into it during the build. As you weave under, over, in and out, the cells or fibres in the wood are reorganized by the pressure you create with your hands. When a rod is first placed and folded against another, that is where it wants to stay. Positive decision-making and precise handling of the material is key to producing a fluent form and a strong object.

YOUR HANDS

The most important tools of all and most commonly used are your hands. They do almost everything. Your hands, along with time and experience, combine to create a dialogue between you and the material. When working with a natural material, practice and repetition are the only ways to understand this language. Fluency in technique and a balanced form come through practice. To keep a round basket round or a square basket square, the newcomer to willow will have to make many baskets.

CREATING THE FORM

Using the correct thickness of material in the right place with the appropriate spaces in between is important. The two general rules are that the frame you are weaving around needs to be thicker than the willow you are weaving with, and the spacing of the frame needs to be close enough for the weaving to be tight. If your weaving is loose the rods need to be thicker, or your frame needs to be closer together. So when you are selecting your material you need to be critical of the spaces and thicknesses chosen in relation to the object to be

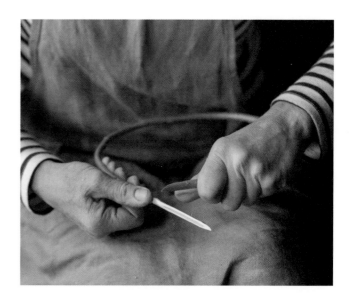

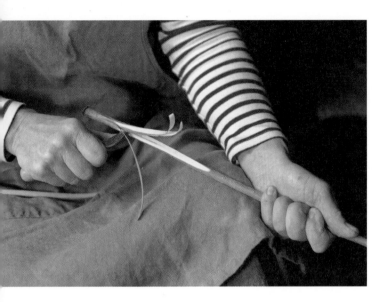

be lying firmly across the top of your knee, allowing the hand holding the knife to operate safely in the area of your lap. It's important to pay attention to how much pith is showing in the rod when you cut, particularly for the long slype, as cutting the correct gradient on the cut is essential for a strong join.

WEAVING PROCESSES

This book is designed to inspire the newcomer to willow. Basket making is a simple craft in that it does not require complex machinery. However, it is a craft that can only be understood thoroughly through repetition. Developing skill with a sharp knife takes time and practice, and I have designed the projects in this book with this in mind. I have used techniques that need little knife work, so that you can get involved in weaving willow more immediately.

The base, sides and border of a basket are intrinsically connected. The border, or rim, is made with the stakes that are woven into the base and travel up the sides. The stakes hold the shape of the basket as you weave around them to make the sides. No one element of this object is separate from the other, they all interconnect.

IMPORTANT NOTE: I often refer to left and right positions of hands or willow. This instruction is given as if from the maker's viewpoint and not the camera's viewpoint. If you struggle you could turn the book upside down, which means you would then view the images in the same way as the maker. When I teach I regularly ask my students to stand behind me to watch a demonstration as they then see the process from the viewpoint they will use themselves. This often helps.

A selection of slypes (opposite, left to right): short slype; long slype, cut on the belly; long slype, cut on the back; long slype, cut on the side; medium slype.

made. Experience, patience and repetition will help to get to grips with this basket-making language.

TEMPLATES

The templates shown on the following pages are the frames around which you weave, which in turn determine the size and shape of your item. All templates need to be thoroughly dried before use. This can take from three to eight weeks.

CUTTING SLYPES

Willow rods are round, so the area where they meet to join needs to be a flat surface, and this has to be cut into them with a knife. For the projects in this book there are generally two types of cuts repeated throughout: a long slype and a short slype. A slype is a cut of varying length that has a smooth surface and a consistent gradient.

It's essential that you are seated in a safe and comfortable position when cutting. Sit on a low chair, holding the butt of a willow rod in your left hand. You will find that your knee naturally offers a firm brace to lock your hand and rod behind. The rod should

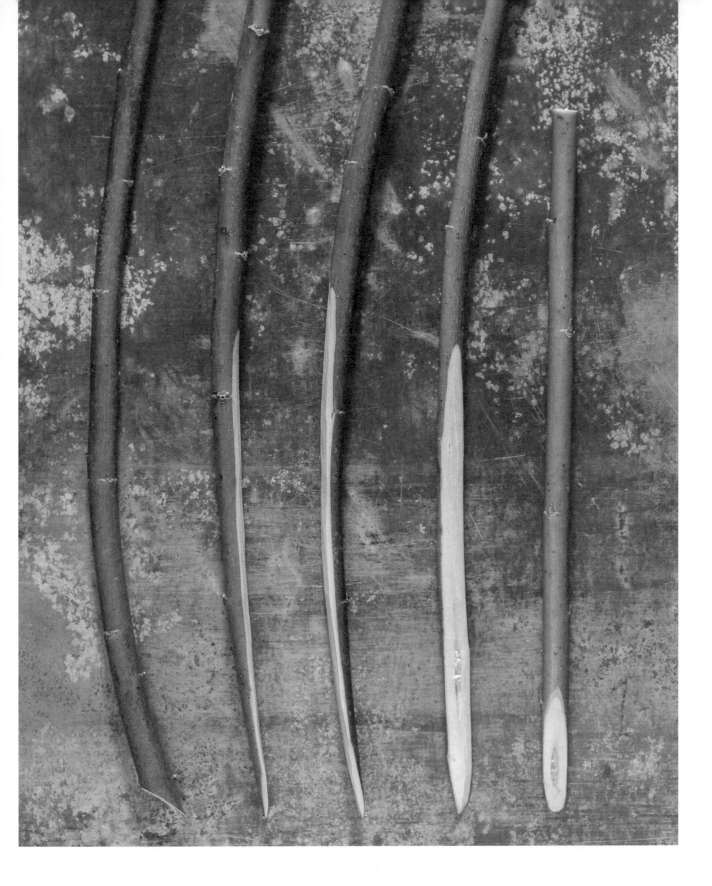

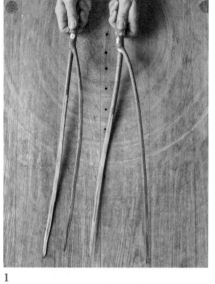

1

2

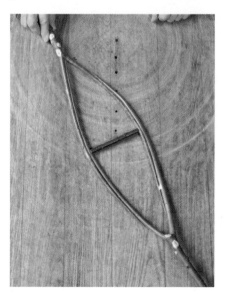

3

NATURAL TEMPLATE

USED FOR: Bread Tray (see page 60) and Fruit Basket (see page 64).

A natural template is made with material that has grown into a forked shape. It doesn't necessarily have to be willow: it can be any type of tree that has a natural Y shape, and is a year or two old. You will need two Y shapes that have generous curves. This template can be made with green, semi-green or soaked material.

STEP 1

Select 2 Y shapes that are similar in weight, length and curve, then cut them to the length suggested in the project. Each of the Y shapes will naturally have a thick and thin rod. Begin by sitting in the safe cutting position and cut a slype on the belly or inside of each of the thicker rods. Cut 2 more slypes on the back or outside of the thin rods. These slypes need to be tapered very gradually over a length of 20–30cm (8–12in) for a seamless join.

The aim is for each side to have a thin and thick length when you slot them together. If your cuts are in the right place then both the thick lengths will sit on the outside of the frame, with the cuts on the belly. This is very important as the thick lengths are stronger and will hold the form.

STEP 2

Before you join the 2 shapes, decide which is the top and which is the bottom, as the template will have its own natural curve. Join 1 side first with Sellotape (Scotch tape) on the 2 ends and in the centre of the slype. If you can't get them to join seamlessly it may be because you have cut them unevenly. Take care to cut in the right place for both surfaces to sit together on the same plane. Join the second side in the same way.

STEP 3

Tap a panel pin through each side in the centre to secure the 2 halves then wedge a dry stick 16–18cm (6–7in) long, cut square at the ends, in the centre of the frame to increase the width. Leave to dry for 6 weeks in the winter and 3 weeks in the summer.

SQUARE TEMPLATE

USED FOR: Trivet (see page 122), Breakfast Tray (see page 126) Jardinière (see page 132), Lunch Bag (see page 136) and Laundry Basket (see page 140).

A square or rectangular basket requires some skill to accomplish. Using this type of template gives the weaver a greater chance of producing a shape that is flat and rigid, with evenly shaped corners. It's important to choose a pair of very straight, green rods of identical thickness that are much longer than the size you need, so that the frame is strong.

1

STEP 1

The joins on the square or rectangular templates in these projects need to be made on the long sides as these are then woven over by the weaving in the base, which makes the joins very secure. After cutting the tips off to the required length lay both rods on a bench to find the back and the belly. The rods will naturally roll onto their sides, which will show you where the back and belly are. For the template to be flat it's important to mark and fold directly on the back of the rod, otherwise your template will not sit flat.

2

STEP 2

For this step I use the tip of the blade of my curved basket maker's knife, but the point of a bodkin will also work. Push the knife halfway through the rod and lift the butt end to a right angle. As you lift, twist the knife. This splits the rod, pushing the fibres sideways, so the rod can bend to a right angle without cracking on the outside edge. Repeat these kinks on the other 3 rods, taking care to kink up directly on the back of the rods.

3

STEP 3

To join the 2 rods together cut 2 slypes 20–30cm (8–12in) long on the back of the rods at the butt end. Cut 2 more long slypes at the tip end on the belly. Join thick to thin with Sellotape (Scotch tape), checking that your joining sides are of equal length. The thick butt ends should be on the outside, with the cut on the inside, or belly. This gives strength and a straight edge.

STEP 4

Tap pins through the centre of both joins. I attach a couple of thin willow ties to the frame to help keep it square while it dries. You can also use string. Leave to dry for 6 weeks in the winter and 3 weeks in the summer, then cut away the tie.

4

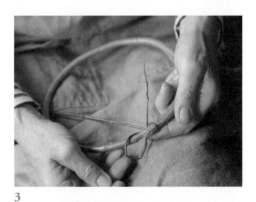

ROUND TEMPLATE

USED FOR: Gathering Basket (see page 68), Wreath (see page 94) and Waste-paper Bin (see page 114).

For the round template a smooth, green rod is an advantage. It can be made with soaked material, but the propensity to kink is greater. For good joins on round templates they need to measure 25 per cent of the circumference of the template.

STEP 1

Sliding the belly of the rod over your knee is essential to achieve a good circle. The idea is to stretch the fibres or cells of the rod on the back by pulling smoothly with some force around your knee. To make a good circle more force needs to go into the thicker end, as it is stronger. If you did not do this and just joined it without prior encouragement, your hoop would naturally make an oval. Some practice will be necessary, as it will take a while to get used to this technique.

STEP 2

With secateurs, cut the rod to the required length, measuring from the butt end. In the safe cutting position cut the first slype at the butt end on the belly. Then cut the adjoining part of the slype at the other end on the back. Encourage the hoop back into a round shape and cross and join the 2 slypes, making sure that the butt end sits on the outside of the circle.

STEP 3

Secure the butt end first with Sellotape (Scotch tape), by placing it right at the end of the cut. This will avoid distortion. Then secure the tip end. Tap a panel pin directly through the middle of the join. The round template needs to be tied to stop it from springing open as it dries. Use string, or tie it with a thin, soaked or fine green rod, looping it over the butt join as shown.

STEP 4

Secure the other end of the tie on the opposite side of the circle in the exact position shown – this is so the template will keep its shape and not distort while it dries. Leave to dry for 6 weeks in the winter and 3 weeks in the summer, then cut away the tie.

START WEAVE

USED FOR: Star (see page 46), Fish (see page 5), Bread Tray (see page 60), Fruit Basket (see page 64), Gathering Basket (see page 68).

Start weave is a method of weaving 2 single sticks together, or starting on a frame that begins with a point, as demonstrated here on the Star template. It also introduces you to the way the pattern evolves as you begin to weave with a material that tapers from thick to thin.

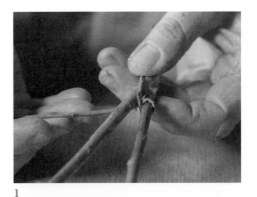

1

STEP 1

Lay the tip of your weaver (the rod you are weaving with) through the apex of the taped Star frame (see page 46), then wrap the tip around the frame to sit on top of the weaver in between the 2 sticks. Hold this firmly with your thumb while using the other hand to continue weaving the second row in a figure of 8 around the frame

STEP 2

For your third row, fold the tip forward so it lies against the frame and so becomes secured as you continue weaving. Continue to weave under and over, from left to right until the rod runs out, taking care to be sensitive to the tension needed to wrap around the frame smoothly. If your movement is firm and positive you will achieve some fluency.

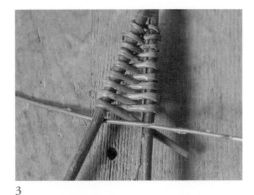

3

STEP 3

When you reach the butt end, tuck it through the frame and allow it to sit in place. To start a new weaver, place the tip on the opposite side of the frame to where your butt ended. To achieve a rhythm in the pattern, weave 3, 5 or 7 rows, then the butts will end on alternate sides. As the template widens increase the thickness of your weaving rod. This helps to create a strong structure by filling the space.

STEP 4

As you come to the end of the frame it becomes increasingly difficult to weave without kinking the willow. Try to make as big a circle as possible with the weaver. This will help you slide the rod into an increasingly tight space. To finish, trim all the protruding tips and butts with secateurs. To get a good, close cut, hold the secateurs at a low angle against the rod, with the blade closest to the weave and lift the rod slightly so that when you cut it springs back into place in the frame and is as snug as possible.

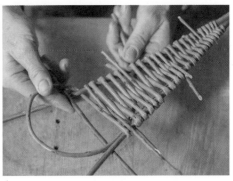

4

1

2

3

THREE-ROD WALE

USED FOR: Cloche (see page 102), Coracle Seat (see page 108), Waste-paper Bin (see page 114), Breakfast Tray (see page 126), Jardinière (page 132), Lunch Bag (see page 136) and Laundry Basket (see page 140).

A Three-rod Wale is a band of weaving that sits at the base and at the top of a basket. At the base, it is an essential method to hold your uprights or stakes in place. Repeated again at the top of your basket it makes a firm structure for you to weave your border onto. It is woven around upright stakes, either woven into a base, as shown here for the Waste-paper Bin, or wedged into the ground or a heavy pot to hold them in place.

STEP 1

A completed Three-rod Wale uses 12 rods. Starting with the tips, take 3 rods and place each behind 3 consecutive stakes. Approximately 20cm (8in) of your tips should point to your left and the rest of the butt end will be pointing to your right. Repeat on the opposite side.

STEP 2

From 1 group of 3, lift the left-hand rod over the top of the remaining 2 and allow it to travel to the right in front of 2 stakes, then place it behind the third stake. Repeat this with the next 2 rods. Continue with the group until you are close to the opposite set of 3, then stop. Continue with the second set of 3 until you meet the first set, and so on. It's important not to weave over the top of a set, but work them both at the same time until the rods run out at the butt end. You should now have 2 sets of 3 butts ending opposite each other.

STEP 3

You now need to add the remaining 6 weavers to complete the sequence. To replace the first set of 3, use a new weaver. Pull back the left-hand butt in the group and slide the new butt end in alongside it. Weave in front of 2 stakes and behind 1. Repeat with a second replacement and then a third replacement weaver. You now have a new set of 3. Continue to weave until you meet the second set of 3 butts, and then repeat the join with your remaining 3 rods.

STEP 4

Weave on with your 2 new sets of 3 until they run out at the tips. They should finish on opposite sides to give you an even band of weaving at the base of your basket. Beat down the weaving with the beater until it is a level height.

4

ENGLISH RAND

1

USED FOR: Cloche (see page 102), Coracle Seat (see page 108), Waste-paper Bin (see page 114), Breakfast Tray (see page 126), Jardinière (page 132), Lunch Bag (see page 136) and Laundry Basket (see page 140).

Rand is a little-used word in the English language. Centuries ago in Dutch and German it meant 'edge'. It means the same in a basket-making context today. There are many different ways of building up the side of a basket – your choice depends of the size of weavers you have available and how tall you would like the side of your basket to be. The English rand technique is a simple weave that shows the tip-to-butt tapering of the rods beautifully. A rand is always built on top of a wale. If you were to begin weaving your sides directly onto your stakes without a wale, you would find it hard to control the shape, and the join with the base and your sides would be very weak.

2

STEP 1

Starting anywhere on the circumference of your basket, lay a single rod behind a stake with the butt end pointing towards the left and on the outside of the basket. Weave in and out of each stake towards the right until the tip meets the place where the butt started.

STEP 2

Repeat Step 1, but start by placing a second butt onto the next stake to the right of the first one you used. As with the first weaver, weave in and out of 1 stake at a time until you meet where your second butt started. Continue with this pattern. Each time you have woven in 4 weavers tap down your weaving with the beater. This will make the weaving tight, give it a strong structure and show off the beauty of the pattern. When you are halfway round your rand will look very uneven in height. Don't panic: it will become level when the pattern is complete.

STEP 3

The pattern is complete when you have a butt protruding from every stake. So if you have 30 stakes you will use 30 weavers. Also, at this stage it's worth checking that the height of the basket is level all the way round before you move on. Beat it down if necessary. It will take some time and practice to be able to create a perfectly round and evenly woven basket

3

FIVE-PAIR BORDER

USED FOR: Waste-paper Bin (see page 114), Breakfast Tray (see page 126), Jardinière (see page 132), Lunch Bag (see page 136) and Laundry Basket (see page 140).

A border is the rim at the top of a basket, and it is created with the stakes. These stakes are woven into the base, travel up the side of the basket and fold down to make the border, so these three elements – the base, sides and top – are all locked in together. This mean the basket cannot fall apart. There are many types of border, but the projects in this book use a Five-pair Border.

STEP 1

Starting anywhere on the top of the basket, use your fingernail or pliers to kink 6 rods to a right angle 1cm (½in) high.

STEP 2

Fold the first kinked rod down, laying it behind the next 2 stakes to the right. Repeat this movement 5 times.

STEP 3

Take the first rod you laid down, pass it in front of 4 stakes to the right in the shape of a bird's wing, then behind the 5th stake.

STEP 4

Bring down the next upright stake by travelling behind 2 stakes to join it with the first to make your first pair. Lay them side by side in the gap. Use your left hand to hold back the next 2 stakes, leaving your right hand free to select the next horizontal stake. Repeat Steps 3 and 4 until you have 5 pairs.

STEP 5

Starting with the first pair, take the right-hand rod forward, continuing to make the shape of a bird's wing. The left-hand rod of the pair is now redundant, so move it away to the left of your body. Then bring down the next stake to make the next pair.

STEP 6

Continue this pattern until you come back to where you started. To finish the border, imagine that the stakes are still upright and what route they would take. The last but one stake still has to travel behind 2, but you need to create a smooth curve to slide it into position, passing it in from the back to the front.

STEP 7

When you take the next horizontal rod to make its pair, this needs to be fed in between the first 2 rods you laid down in Step 2. You then have your pair. The spaces are very tight so use your bodkin. This leaves 1 more gap with no pairs.

STEP 8

Repeat Steps 6 and 7 with the last upright and the next horizontal. You now have 4 pairs left to finish.

STEP 9

Continue to take the right-hand rod of each pair and thread it between what were the upright stakes, but thread it so it comes out underneath the bird's-wing shape. When the border is complete, use the secateurs to trim all the ends of your stakes that stick out from underneath the border, as close as you can to the weave.

1

2

3

4

5

6

7

8

9

PROJECTS

HERE ARE A FEW TECHNICAL TIPS THAT WILL BE USEFUL FOR ALL OF THE PROJECTS. WILLOWS VARY ACCORDING TO VARIETY AND CONDITION, SO ALL THE SUGGESTED THICKNESSES WILL BE IN RELATION TO THE TYPE OF WILLOW.

When I have given quantities of stakes and weavers, they are based on the willow I use. Yours may be a little fatter or thinner, so you may need more or less than I have suggested. It is always advisable to soak more willow than you need to accommodate these variables.

When a three-dimensional weave is complete, the firm way it once sat on the board has often changed and it might be a little wobbly. Before the basket dries out, manipulate it back into a level shape. Think of yourself as a chiropractor: you are simply encouraging the frame to return back to its original plane.

Finally, once a piece is made it's important to place it somewhere dry and airy for approximately five days for it to dry out thoroughly, otherwise some mould can appear.

CHAPTER ONE

FLAT WEAVE

Flat-weave techniques are used in many ways in many cultures, largely to create panels for dividing or screening spaces indoors and outdoors. Building houses, partitioning rooms and containing animals are all functions for which flat weave is utilized. The projects in this chapter are designed to be simple so that you can concentrate on becoming familiar with the fundamental patterns of weaving with a material that is fat at one end and thin at the other. The different shapes will help you to understand why you need patterns of weaving, and how those patterns contribute to a balanced and secure object that is also visually pleasing.

STAR

WHAT YOU NEED

for a star with a 30cm (12in) diameter

For the template:

5 dry willow sticks of identical thickness, as
straight as you can find, 5mm (³/₈in) thick at
the butt

For the weaving:

soaked or semi-green willow, approximately
20 rods 50–70cm (20–28in) long

Tools:

secateurs, Sellotape (Scotch tape)

THE STAR IS A SIMPLE PROJECT to start with, as the template is made from dry willow sticks
and so can be used straight away. The weaving introduces you to the principles of how to build a pattern into
a space that starts off small and opens out into a larger space. In doing this you will also become aware of
the importance of using the different lengths and thicknesses of willow that you will find in one bundle.

A willow star makes a lovely, simple gift, particularly at Christmas. Hung on a wall or in a window, a
star symbolizes that classic festive imagery, the star of Bethlehem, and so is a traditional welcoming sign for
visitors. Willow stars also lend themselves to being a flat centrepiece on a table, with a candle holder in the
middle, or dressed with seasonal vegetation, such as ivy or mistletoe.

1

STEP 1

Cut the 5 sticks to 30cm (1ft) long, making sure they are all exactly the same length. Take 4 sticks, separate them into pairs and tape the pairs together at one end. Weave these 2 pairs together, under and over, making 3 of the 5 points of the star. When in place the frame will become locked together.

2

STEP 2

To make the remaining points of the star, add your fifth stick, weaving under and over the frame. Before you tape the remaining 3 points together make sure they sit in an opposite position to the way they have crossed in the centre. This makes your star frame very secure. If you find your fifth stick kinks when you insert it, it may mean that the sticks chosen for this size frame are too thick. If so, try choosing a thinner set. Take into account where the back and the belly lie on each stick – you may have to roll some of the rods to sit more comfortably within the star frame. You are now ready to weave.

STEP 3

Choose the shortest and finest rod to start your weave. Weave 1 rod into each of the 5 points. (See Start Weave, page 37.) This helps to keep an even tension. If you were to weave a whole point of the star before the others, you would find it hard to achieve a balanced shape.

3

STEP 4

The number of rods used to fill the space depends on how large your star is. Increase the length and thickness of the rod you weave with as the gap gets wider. Continue until the 5 points are filled. Use secateurs to trim all the ends close to the frame. You could you also fill the centre of the star if you wanted.

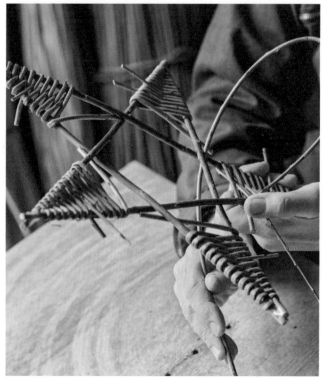

4

FISH

WHAT YOU NEED
to make a fish approximately 30cm (1ft)
  in length

For the template:
soaked or semi-green willow, 1 rod 180cm (6ft)
  long, 7.5mm (¹/₃in) thick at the butt
1 dry stick 30cm (1ft) long, 7.5mm (¹/₃in) thick at
  the butt

For the weaving:
soaked or semi-green willow,
  12 rods 60–100cm (2–3ft) long

Tools:
basket maker's knife, secateurs, Sellotape
  (Scotch tape), panel pins, pin hammer,

THE WEAVING PATTERNS that we explored in the Star (see page 46) are also used in this project. But this template is made with a fresh piece of willow, so you can get a feel for how to make curved shapes of your choice, in this case a fish.

Somehow this simple project holds tremendous historical significance in my mind. It's thought that the symbolism of the fish has its origins as far back as the 4th-century BC, and it has been used by the Christian faith in art and architecture. Even today you see it represented widely as a symbol of faith and peace. I believe its importance, in a time when drawing materials were little used, is due to readily available natural materials, such as willow, lending themselves to this simple template and weave.

1

2

3

STEP 1

To make your template, make a mark 35cm (1ft) up from the butt end on the belly of the rod. Use a knife to kink the willow to create the nose of the fish. (See Step 1 of Square Template, page 35.)

STEP 2

Cross the 2 lengths at a point that gives you the shape of a fish. The thicker part of the rod will want to stay straighter than the thin. Encourage the fibres to stretch and give, to create more of a curve (see Step 1 of Round Template, page 36.) When you are happy with the shape tape the cross and tap in a panel pin.

STEP 3

Push a length of dry stick into the body part of the fish. It should be a tight enough fit to wedge itself in place. This helps to judge the shape of the tail before weaving. To finish and secure the template, kink the tip end of the rod to a right angle to form the corner of the tail. Make your first wrap of weaving around the end of the butt on the other side. Continue to weave around the frame part of the tail towards the body until the tip runs out. Allow to dry before weaving.

Turn the fish around to begin weaving the nose of the fish, starting with the shortest rods. (See Start Weave, page 37.) If your weaving starts to feel loose introduce a longer, and consequently thicker, rod as the gap to weave gets wider. When you have woven in 2 or 3 rods you can get rid of the dry stick, as the weaving will hold the frame. Continue to weave the rest of the body.

STEP 4

As the template narrows towards the tail, use shorter, thinner rods. When you get to the template cross, wrap the join once as tightly as you can and then continue to weave into the tail section until it's completely filled.

STEP 5

Remember to increase the size of the weavers again as the tail widens. Trim all the ends as close to the frame as you can.

4

5

SCREEN

WHAT YOU NEED

For the frame:

4 half-round chestnut poles 1m (3ft) long

4 coach bolts

4 thick sticks of willow or hazel 1m (3ft) long

4 cable ties 35cm (1ft) long

8 screws 5cm (2in) long

For the weaving:

dry, soaked or semi-green willow, approximately

  260 rods at least

  150cm (5ft) long

Tools:

drill, spanner, screwdriver, beater, bodkin, secateurs

THE IDEA BEHIND THIS PROJECT is to make a 1m- (3ft-) square panel that can be used to screen or divide an area in your garden. A larger panel could be made in exactly the same way, but for strength you would need to weave with bigger willow. I have used half-round chestnut posts for the frame because I live near a fencing company that manufactures riven and split chestnut poles. But other wooden material you may have at hand, such as flat planks, could also work to make the frame.

    The weaving pattern in this project will help you to understand how to lay in a natural material that tapers from thick to thin.

1

STEP 1

First we need to construct the frame (see photograph, page 54). On the ground, lay out the half-round chestnut poles in a square, flat side to flat side. Mark and drill the 4 corners and bolt them together using the coach bolts. Attaching the 4 larger sticks comes next, but before you do you need to choose which way to lay them onto the frame so that the panel of weaving is flat. Pay attention to where the back and the belly of the sticks lie. If you have a stick with a very curved back and belly then attach it sideways, otherwise your panel will weave up with a bulge in it. At this point, only screw in the sticks on the bottom of the frame. Mark equal distances, drill pilot holes, then screw the bottom of the larger sticks in place. To temporarily hold the top of the sticks in place use the cable ties. Take care to tie them equal distances apart.

STEP 2

Your frame is ready to weave. As a basket maker I have the advantage of having wooden blocks available for clamping the frame securely while I weave. However, leaning the frame up against a wall will also work. Take a bunch of 6 rods and place the butt ends on the front of the left-hand side of the frame. Weave a row in and out of each stake with all 6 rods. The tips will end on the opposite side of the frame and protrude way beyond it. For your second row, start on the same side but with your butts on the back of the frame. Weave another row. Repeat for the third and fourth rows, but start with your butts on the right-hand side of the frame.

STEP 3

Now alternate these 2 sequences all the way up the panel. Notice the alternate pattern of bunches of butts and tips that develops on the sides of the frame. We know willow is thick at one end and thin at the other, so alternating where to start the rows ensures the panel weaves up level. If you put all of your butts on the same side, the panel would fill up on that side first, leaving the right side thin and open. For a firm and solid fence use your beater to beat down the weaving every 4 rows.

STEP 4

Once you have woven up half the panel you can cut the cable ties off, as your stakes will be firmly positioned in place. This allows you to slide your weavers in between the frame and stakes as the space gets smaller and the weaving gets harder.

STEP 5

When you get to the top, drill pilot holes through the stakes and into the frame before you screw them in place. Then trim all the ends neatly so they sit comfortably on the frame.

2

3

4

5

CHAPTER TWO

NATURAL WEAVE

When we think of a basket we often think of an object that has a base, sides, a border and a handle. The projects in this chapter have none of these elements: they are built in a very different way. I have called this chapter 'Natural Weave' because the shapes of the templates and the forms are created by the natural growth that occurs in the material chosen. This way of working is less formal. One of the most beautiful aspects is that the templates used simply reflect the organic curves that nature readily provides. The templates don't necessarily have to be willow – they could be harvested from any type of tree that gives this Y shape. From these templates you can easily change the shape by adding more 'ribs' to the framework, which increases the volume.

Woven shapes of this construction have been used for centuries by farm workers, who would weave up baskets during the winter months for use in the summer. This method gives a very strong framework around which to weave. It also allows you to stop and start weaving more freely than the conventional way, when you are often working quite quickly to complete the border before the material dries out. My belief is that this type of free-form basket would have been the ancestor of the more complicated construction widely used today.

For the Fruit Basket I demonstrate how to wrap a rod around a wooden pole to help you thread it into a limited space when completing the weave (see Step 5, page 67). This is a useful technique that can be applied to many of the other projects in this book.

BREAD TRAY

WHAT YOU NEED

For the template:
Natural Template (see page 34) – 80cm (2½ft)
  long and 20cm (8in) wide, made from thick
  green or semi-green willow, hazel, ash or beech,
  1.75cms (²/₃in) thick at the butt, then dried
  before use

For the weaving:
soaked or semi-green willow, approximately 35
  rods 120–180cm (4–6ft) long
2 dry sticks 70cm (28in) long, 7.5mm (¹/₃in) thick
  at the butt

Tools:
basket maker's knife, Sellotape (Scotch tape), pin
  hammer, panel pins, beater, bodkin, secateurs,
  a bottle/wooden pole to wrap the final weavers
  around for flexibility, saw

FLAT, WOVEN SHAPES SUCH AS THIS have been used for centuries by farmers in the Mediterranean for drying fruit and vegetables. At harvest time fruits such as figs, tomatoes, apricots and grapes were laid out on these trivets in the full sun to dry. The design allowed the air to move freely around the produce for drying. Sometimes the trays were so large that two people were needed to carry them.

This Bread Tray will bear the temperature of a hot dish straight from the oven and so can also work well as a trivet or centrepiece on a table laid for a dinner party, or for presenting warm bread or croissants at breakfast. Or, indeed, if you are a keen gardener and are lucky enough live in a Mediterranean climate, you could dry your own produce.

STEP 1

Retain the dry stick in the centre of the Natural Template to hold the width of the template. Starting with the shortest of the weavers, begin weaving as described in Start Weave (see page 37). For this trivet it can look nice if you wrap your weaver around the frame twice as you weave. Weave 2 or 3 rods into each end.

Decide which is the top and which is the bottom of your frame by placing it on a flat surface to see which way up it sits most comfortably. Notice in your weaving that the gaps are getting bigger and bigger quite quickly as the frame widens. You have created 2 natural 'pockets' to insert 2 stakes. These need to be thicker than the weavers, but thinner than the frame. Cut a short slype on the side of both stakes at the butt end and push them into the spaces very firmly. To repeat at the other end, cut the stakes 1.5cm (½in) longer than the space so they overlap onto the weaving. Cut a slype on the side of both stakes. Take a stake and gently encourage it into a curve – this will shorten the length so you are able to firmly push it into the weaving at the other end of the frame. Repeat with the second stake. The stakes should be flat and feel very secure. If you didn't add these, your weaving would become looser as you weave into the wider part of the frame.

1

STEP 2

Adding these stakes changes your weaving pattern. You now have 4 rods to weave around instead of 2. To start the new pattern position the butt of the last weaver on top of the frame. Begin the next weaver by laying the tip directly underneath the frame where the previous butt ended. Continue to weave, wrapping once or twice around the frame, using the pattern described in Start Weave (see page 37). Remember to weave an odd number of rows – 3, 5 or 7 – with each rod. The pattern will then grow with a butt ending on alternate sides, giving rhythm and fluency to the weave. As the basket increases in width use longer and longer rods. To avoid distortion weave into each end alternately until the weavers meet in the middle. When you have woven about a third of each end, you can push out the dry stick that holds the width of the basket. It's worth tapping the weave with your beater after every couple of rows as this helps to increase the density of the weave, which in turn increases the strength of the basket.

2

STEP 3

Continue to weave this pattern. You should find that all of your butts end up underneath the frame and all of your tips sit on the top. As the 2 sides of weaving meet and the gap gets smaller, it gets harder and harder to handle the willow. With your weaver, try make as big a circle as possible to help you slide the rod in and out of the decreasing space.

3

STEP 4

As the 2 sides of weaving come together, you need to consider the very last row of weaving. It may fall into the same pattern as the other side, giving a double row. To avoid this, squeeze the weaving a little tighter with the bodkin so you are able to add another row, which will hold the pattern of the 2 sides as they meet. Trim all the ends of the weavers at the top and bottom as close as you dare. Then, with a saw, cut both ends of the template to suit.

4

FRUIT BASKET

WHAT YOU NEED

For the template:
Natural Template (see page 34) – 70cm (28in) long
and 16cm (6in) wide, made from green or semi-
green willow, hazel, ash or beech, 1.25cms ($^{1}/_{2}$in)
thick at the butt, then dried before use

For the weaving:
soaked or semi-green willow, approximately 35 rods
100–150cm (3–5ft) long

For the ribs:
soaked or semi-green willow, 4 rods 50cm (1$^{1}/_{2}$ft)
long, 7.5mm ($^{1}/_{3}$in) thick at the butt

Tools:
basket maker's knife, Sellotape (Scotch tape), pin
hammer, panel pins, bodkin, secateurs, beater,
a bottle/wooden pole to wrap the final weavers
around for flexibility, saw

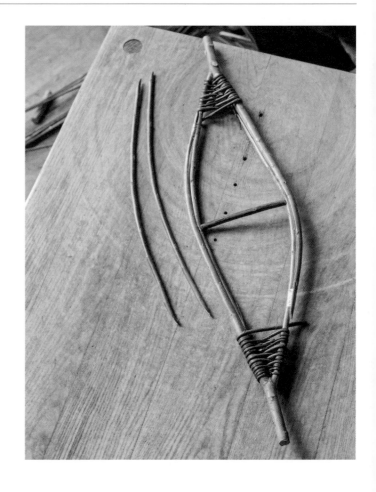

THIS PROJECT USES THE SAME techniques as the Bread Tray (see page 60), but shows you how you can lengthen and increase the number of stakes to change a basket that is flat into one that is three-dimensional. We are adding four soaked ribs instead of dry ones in this design. You could easily increase the volume and depth of the piece by adding more stakes as ribs.

This simple, natural form is perfect for displaying any kind of fruit or vegetables. It works well on a window sill, sideboard or as a table centre. Because the template is made from two natural Y shapes the basket takes on the shape of the tree from which it was cut, so remember that this type of template can come in all shapes and sizes.

1

2

3

STEP 1

Retain the dry stick in your Natural Template. Begin weaving as described in Start Weave (see page 37) and continue until you have 2 or 3 weavers in each end. The edge of the basket looks better if you wrap the weaver around the template twice as you weave. Next you need to create the belly of the basket by inserting the first pair of stakes by following Step 1 in Bread Tray (see page 62). However, for this project the stakes need to be soaked or semi-green, as they have to make a deeper curve and would crack if they were dry. Once the butt ends are in place, cut the stakes 2–4cm (¾–1½in) longer than the length of the space between the weaving – this will dictate how deep the basket will be. Pay attention to the hand positions and tension used to insert the curved stake.

STEP 2

Now you have 2 stakes as well as the frame to weave around, so the pattern of weaving changes. The weaving ended with a butt, so start the next weaver with a tip, laying it in the position shown. Weave 2 or 3 more weavers at each end.

STEP 3

As you weave, the space between the new stakes and the frame gets bigger: these gaps are the ones you use to add another pair of stakes, cutting slypes and inserting them in the same way as you did the first 2. Once all 4 stakes are in, check that the curves are all in the right place. The central pair should sit level on a surface and the second pair should hold identical curves. If you cut the stake too short the form will be too flat and if you cut them too long the form will have a protruding lump. To adjust this you can ease the stake in or out of its seating until it looks and feels right and even. You will have to do this several time as you continue to weave. Once a larger proportion of the basket is woven the stakes will stop moving.

STEP 4

Now you have 4 stakes and the frame to weave around. Again, this changes the pattern of weaving. This time, position the last butt to sit on the inside of the basket on 1 of the middle pairs of stakes. Add in the next weaver, tip first, so that it sits underneath where the butt ended and weave back in the same direction. On the first row you will find that the new weaver will momentarily follow the same path as the previous weaver. This is part of the pattern. The rest of the basket is woven in this pattern, bearing in mind the principle of weaving an odd number of rows so that the butts can finish alternately on the centre pair of stakes, giving your basket an even flow. Continue this pattern of weaving. This means that all of your butts should end up sitting alternately on the central pair of stakes on the inside of the basket and the tips should end up starting in the same place, but on the outside of the basket. Carry on weaving a few rods on each side until you get to the middle, increasing the length of the weavers as you go. Discard the central stick.

STEP 5

As the space gets smaller and smaller it may be helpful to wrap the weavers around a bottle or wooden pole first. This helps to encourage the fibres in the rod to stretch to allow a curve. It can help tremendously when you are weaving the last few rods into a small gap. It helps you make big circles without kinking while you are weaving into such a tight space.

STEP 6

To avoid a double row in the centre, squeeze the weaving a little tighter with the bodkin so you are able to add another row. Trim all the ends sitting inside and outside the basket. Cut the ends of the frame to length with a saw, and with your knife, tidy up any knobbly bits on the stems. To encourage this basket to sit level you can push down quite heavily on the frame to reseat the weaving to help balance the form. This needs to done while the willow is still wet. Once dry everything will be rigid.

4

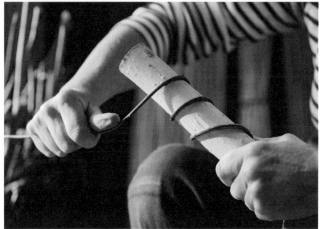

5

6

GATHERING BASKET

For the template:

4 Round Templates (see page 36) – 2 x 18cm (7in)
diameter and 7.5mm ($^1/_3$in) thick at the butt, 2 x
32cm (12$^1/_2$in) diameter and 1cm ($^1/_2$in) thick at
the butt, made from green or semi-green willow,
then dried before use

For the weaving:

soaked or semi-green willow,
6 sticks 70cm (28in) long, 1cm ($^1/_2$in) thick at the
butt for the ribs
10 rods 120cm (4ft) long
10 rods 150cm (5ft) long
50 rods 180cm (6ft) long

Tools:

basket maker's knife, Sellotape (Scotch tape), pin
hammer, panel pins, bodkin, secateurs, beater,
a bottle/wooden pole to wrap the final weavers
around for flexibility

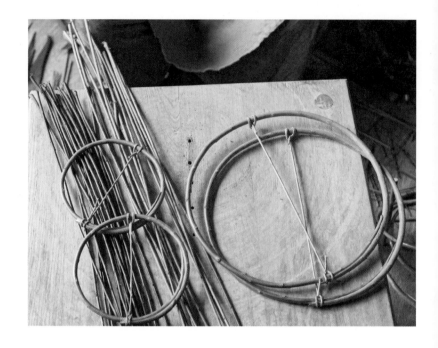

THIS BASKET BEGINS WITH four round templates that meet and make the handle. The large
templates form the base on which the basket sits firmly on a surface and the small templates create the
opening for the handle. For my basket I added six ribs, but if you wanted to make a basket with a greater
volume you could add more ribs. I have seen some very old photographs of groups of ladies chatting in a
French market while proudly holding some very large, stunning versions of this basket.

Everybody's grandmother had one of these in the 1940s and '50s, and they were carried to town
to hold the grocery shopping. You see them a lot in antiques shops, and they carry fond memories for many
of us. I have called mine a Gathering Basket, as it's the perfect size for the keen vegetable gardener to harvest
enough for a family feast.

1

STEP 1

Lay the 4 templates on top of each other, with the 2 small frames on the outside. It's very important not to have any of the template joins at the top where the handle is going to be. Also, to be sure that the weight of the frames is balanced, place the joins of the templates in opposite directions, as shown.

STEP 2

When you are happy with the positions, draw a mark on all the templates to establish where the centre of the handle will be, and put some tape either side of this. Line up all the marks and tap a long panel pin directly through all of the hoops at this point. This helps to secure the 4 templates so you can start to weave.

STEP 3

Using 2 of the shortest rods, link the tips around each other and lay that join on the marks made.

STEP 4

With 1 of the rods, begin to wrap around all 4 templates as tightly and as neatly as you can manage, trapping the tip of the rod inside your wrapping as you go.

STEP 5

Wrap 1 rod several times until you have 25cm (10in) of the rod left. To secure this rod, part the 2 large templates by squeezing them apart over your knee. This will create a gap wide enough for you to secure the butt firmly between the 2 large templates.

STEP 6

Repeat with the second rod, working in the other direction. There's a lot to keep control of at this stage, so I use tape to add some dry spacing sticks to help retain the shape as I weave.

STEP 7

You now work on separating the 4 templates into 2 pairs. Still using the short weavers, tuck the tip into the place where the previous butt ended. Think of the weaver as a continuous length of weaving: this will help you understand where to place it. As you weave with the thin end of this new rod, start to separate the templates into 4 by squeezing the weaver between the large and small templates. The aim is to separate all 4 templates with

2

3

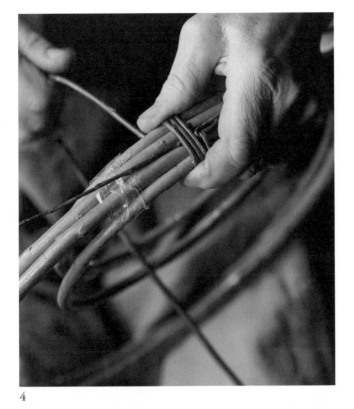

4

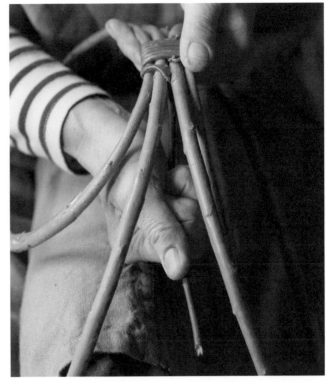

5

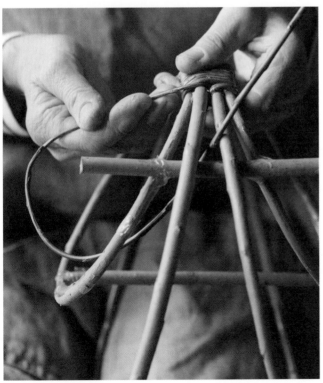

6

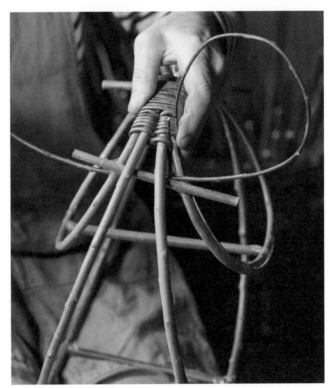

7

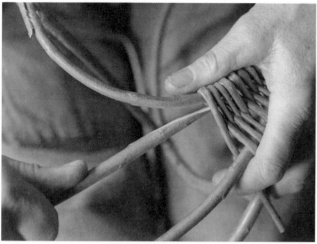

8

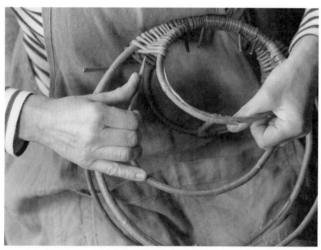

9

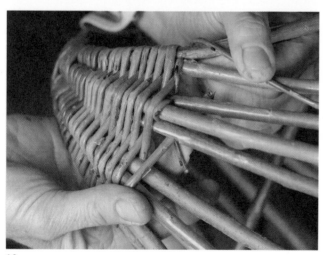

10

the weaver. Turn it around and repeat on the other side of the handle. Continue to weave on both sides with the remaining shortest weavers. For this shape it's hard to find a regular pattern for your weaving. The only rule is not to have butts or tips ending or starting on the small round templates as this is the edge of the basket, and they would be vulnerable.

STEP 8

When you have woven all 10 rods you will find that the gaps between the templates have widened, which gives you room in your weave to add more frame. You need 6 ribs to fill the spaces to be woven – an extra 2 in each of the 3 spaces. On the butt end of one of the sticks cut a short slype on the belly and insert this rib into the weaving next to the small template. This is when your bodkin comes in handy. If you can't get the slip into the weave easily, push the bodkin in firmly and wiggle it about. The rod will now go in much more easily.

STEP 9

Judge the length you need to make the first rib by offering it up to the weaving on the opposite side of the basket and cut a second slype on the belly. Insert that into the weaving on the other side, again using the bodkin if necessary. You will need to do a little shaping and moulding to encourage the rib to curve evenly. (See Step 1 of Round Template, page 36.) Add in the remaining 5 ribs on either side of each of the large templates.

STEP 10

Continue to weave with the finest of the 150cm (5ft) rods, again starting with the tip in the exact place where the butt finished. Weave under and over all the templates and newly added ribs, encouraging them all to separate as you go. This will feel very tight to begin with. The only pattern is when you add in a new weaver: always start with the tip and weave out to the butt. I always keep my joins on the inside of the basket as it looks a lot neater. Weave 5 rods on the first side and then 5 on the other side to help to keep the form even. As the gaps get larger, move on to weaving with the thicker 180cm (6ft) rods and remember to tap with your beater every so often; this will keep the basket strong.

STEP 11

When you have woven a number of rows you will notice that the small hoops are being woven up more rapidly than the larger part of the basket. At this stage we need to change the weaving pattern to ensure that the larger part of the basket is filled. To do this you weave a shorter row. So instead of weaving to the small template you weave to the outer rib only and then turn back to weave to the other side. On the next row you weave back and forth to the second rib only; on the third row you weave up to the 2 larger templates only. Then you weave back up to the small template again and repeat.

11

STEP 12

You will notice that by using this pattern the larger volume of the basket will begin to fill more quickly without cramming up the space on the small templates. Continue to do this until you have an even strap of unwoven basket. When the 2 sides have been woven evenly, return to the original weave pattern of weaving all the way across from small template to small template to complete the basket. As the gap gets smaller it gets harder to weave, so refer to Step 5 of Fruit Basket (see page 67) to help you handle the willow in a small space. Try not to have all your butt-to-tip joins in the same place. Weave so the rods start and end in different places: this will keep the weaving strong. To finish, try not to end with a double row. Trim all the ends. Re-set the basket on a flat surface while it is damp so it sits firmly.

12

CHAPTER THREE

SPIRAL WEAVE

The spiral weave, as I have called it, is taken from an ancient technique of folding straw. There are some very elaborate examples of plaiting and braiding straw into decorative and religious objects. One of the most effective is the spiral weave. Straw is a very different material from willow: it is thin, flat and pliable. The projects in this section use the spiral weave, but the method is tailored to the characteristics of willow, being round, thin at one end and fat at the other. The scale of the object made is dictated by the length and the number of the rods chosen. The beauty for me in this project is that the whole of the length of the rod is used, so there is very little waste, and the rhythm of making is continuous from beginning to end. They are a pleasure to weave.

The weaving pattern in the four projects in this chapter is dependant on an extra rod being added at the beginning of the weaving, once the template is set up. When the wooden template is used, it is drilled to hold a number of rods, then an extra one is added to start the pattern. To illustrate this I have used a different-coloured rod as the one that is added; this should be clear in the photographs.

A wooden disc is used for three of the projects. I used a piece of apple wood from the garden, because at the time of writing I had recently severely pruned an apple tree. Any type of wood is suitable to make the disc for the template, so long as it is soft enough to drill into. But it is essential that the piece of wood is allowed to dry out slowly before use, to avoid it splitting when you drill into it. If you don't have access to pruned trees, it is possible to buy these discs on the internet.

NAPKIN RING

WHAT YOU NEED

For the template:
I disc of dry wood 8cm (3in) in diameter and 2cm
(³/₄in) thick

For the weaving:
soaked or semi-green willow, 6 fine rods
85–100cm (2³/₄–3ft) long

Tools:
drill, Sellotape (scotch tape), bodkin, your knees,
secateurs

THE NAPKIN RING is a simple introduction to the spiral weave. Because it's a small piece it uses lightweight willow. Once you start folding, the willow the pattern builds very quickly and so it is an easy and relatively quick item to make.

These days, the culinary industry is moving more and more towards using not only local produce with a small carbon footprint, but also local and natural materials for presentation. Wood, slate, terracotta, natural fibres and local foliage are all making their way onto our dining tables. These napkin rings are ideal to add to this type of setting, and can be made quite vibrant by varying the colour of willow used. To do this, take care to choose willows that are of a similar length and dimension.

1

STEP 1

Draw a circle on the disc with a 5cm (2in) diameter. Drill 5 holes, at equal distances apart, around the circumference of the circle, using a drill bit of a similar thickness to the willow you are using.

STEP 2

Thread the 5 tips of the rods through the disc so you have at least 25cm (10in) protruding and wrap them together with tape.

STEP 3

On the other side of the disc choose any of the rods to start weaving. Lay in an extra rod (shown as a green willow), and fold your chosen brown rod down to the right, over the top of the green rod and on the inside of the next rod. The green rod sits beneath the first fold on the inside of the rod. Take the second brown rod, fold it over the first and lay it behind the third.

STEP 4

Continue until all rods are folded down. The next row begins with the green rod and will take you on to the next row. For clarity keep an eye on the route the green rod takes.

STEP 5

Fold the added rod firmly upwards and over the top of the fifth rod, to the right. Lay it on top of the next rod to the right.

2

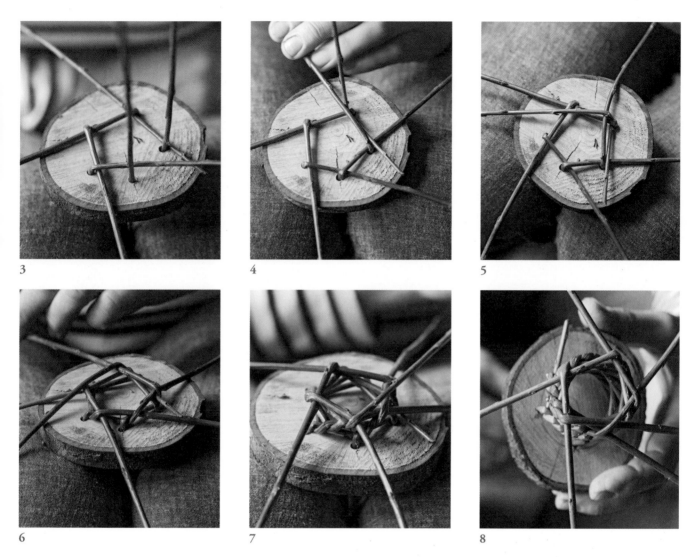

3

4

5

6

7

8

STEP 6

Holding it securely but leaving it behind, pick up the rod underneath it and fold that rod over the top to lay on top of the next one to the right, and so on. So each time you fold and lay a rod on top of the next, you drop that to pick up the rod from underneath to continue. Each time turn the disc clockwise while holding the tips with your knees.

STEP 7

As you move around the circle a spiral pattern appears at the point where you fold. Repeat this sequence until the napkin ring is 6cm (2½in) deep. Take care to keep identical lengths between each fold. It's then time to finish off.

STEP 8

You can stop anywhere in the sequence. Instead of laying the rod on top of the next folding point, thread it underneath and through the weaving below. To do this, remember to make as big a circle as possible to slide this last rod into place. You will find you now have 2 rods in the same space. This is all you need to do to finish this weave. Trim your butt ends.

To take the Napkin Ring out of the block, cut the tape and gently slide the block over the tips. The tips will spring flat. There is no threading to be done here so just trim them neatly too. A little white flash of a clean cut adds to the simplicity and character of the design.

BIRD FEEDER

For the template:

I disc of dry wood 10cm (4in) in diameter and 2cm
(³/₄in) thick

For the weaving:

soaked or semi-green willow, 7 fine rods 180cm
(6ft) long

Tools:

drill, Sellotape (Scotch tape), bodkin, your knees,
secateurs, twine

THE CONSTRUCTION OF THE BIRD FEEDER is very similar to the napkin ring. However, it's a taller and wider basket so the willow is longer and there are more rods. The wooden disc acts as a template, but also remains a part of the object. I like to leave the tips of the willow long at the bottom of the basket as I have noticed that the birds like to use them as platforms to land on.

Since designing this feeder for this book I have used them a lot in my garden and have noticed an increase in bird population. They very quickly become well used, and they really help to introduce you to the birds that live your neighbourhood.

1

STEP 1

Begin with a round wooden disc at least 10cm (4in) in diameter, I used a piece of cherry from the wood pile. Draw a circle with an 8cm (3in) diameter, mark then drill 6 holes equal distances apart. Check your drill bit is slightly bigger than the size of the willow to be used. Start by following Steps 3–7 of Napkin Ring (see pages 78–9), but thread 6 tips through the holes in the wooden disc, leaving 40cm (16in) to spare. You will need to weave with these later on. When you have added the extra rod (shown as a green rod here) you will be weaving with 7 rods.

STEP 2

You will notice as the tube grows in height the willow becomes thicker and the structure becomes stronger. Keep folding until it reaches a height of 12–15cm (5–6in) and finish in the same way as in Napkin Ring (see Step 8, page 79) by curving the rod you choose to be the last underneath the weave. You may need to use the bodkin to make a space. Trim the butts, leaving 5mm (⅜in). This extra length allows for the slight movement there can be with this type of weaving.

2

3

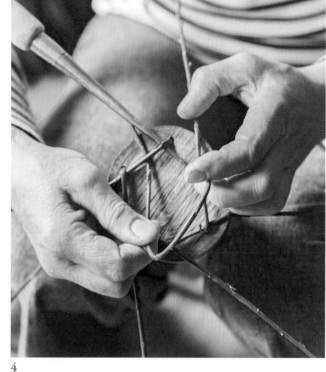

4

STEP 3

To finish, turn the basket upside down and hold it between your knees. Weave 1 round of spiral weave with the tips.

STEP 4

Thread the last rod inwards under the first, folded down, making the sequence complete and secure.

STEP 5

Trim the tips to a length of 10cm (4in) so the birds have more choice in how to approach the feeder. You could leave them longer if you wish. Add several strands of strong twine looped through the top row to suspend it in the garden.

5

EGG BASKET

WHAT YOU NEED

For the template:
I disc of dry wood 12cm (5in) in diameter and 2cm
   (³/₄in) thick

For the weaving:
soaked or semi-green willow, 13 fine rods 150cm
   (5ft) long

Tools:
drill, secateurs, bodkin, Sellotape (scotch tape),
   your knees

THIS EGG BASKET IS MADE using the same spiral weave as in Bird Feeder (see page 80), but this time you drill the holes into the side of the disc of wood instead of the top. I have always thought about making a basket with this spiral technique and so decided to explore the idea so it could be used in this book. It would be tricky to use the technique to make the base, so introducing another natural material that could be used as the base and template seemed a good idea.

This basket is ideal for the quantity of eggs a family may use, and they look so inviting stored in this willow version of a nest.

STEP 1

Mark the outside rim of the wooden disc with 12 marks in the same position as the digits on a clock. Drill a hole into these marks at least 3cm (1in) deep using a drill bit slightly larger than the thin end of your 12 weavers. Cut approximately 25cm (10in) off the tips of the weavers and insert 1 into each of the holes. Put the basket onto a flat surface with a heavy weight inside before you start to weave. Choose 1 of the rods and gently fold it down onto the top of the next rod to the right. Leave that rod behind and pick up the next one, folding it over the first and laying it on top of the third, and so on, until you get to where you started.

1

STEP 2

When you get to where you started you will find that you don't have 1 to fold; this is where you add in number 13. For clarity I have used a brown rod as the 13th rod. Thread it under the first fold just to secure it.

2

STEP 3

Now, when you continue to weave and include the added 1, you will find you will begin to travel over 2 rods, as shown. So when you pick up a new rod it travels to the right over 2 weavers, and with each movement you leave the previous weaver behind. To get on to the next level, just keep weaving in the same way.

3

STEP 4

The shape of this basket depends on where you make your folds. If you wanted a tube you would keep folding directly on top of the fold beneath and keep the length of the folds the same. For the Egg Basket we want the side to angle outwards, so fold slightly to the side of the fold beneath, allowing the length of the fold to increase. To a degree, the increase of the circumference will also happen naturally as your weavers become thicker as you weave towards the butts. Continue to weave until you get to the required depth – mine is 6cm (2½in).

4

STEP 5

As with the Napkin Ring and Bird Feeder (see pages 76 and 80) you can choose any rod to finish. This leaves 1 space with a pair of rods while all the other spaces have only 1 rod. Keep the weight inside the basket until you have finished as this will give much more purchase in order to weave and trim.

5

STEP 6

Using the secateurs, trim the rods, leaving 5mm (⅜in) protruding from the basket. This allows for the slight movement there can be with this type of weaving, and ensures the rods don't slip free.

6

GARLIC HOLDER

WHAT YOU NEED

For the weaving:
soaked or semi-green willow, 9 very slender rods
  180cm (6ft) long

Tools:
Sellotape (Scotch tape), bodkin, your knees,
  secateurs, twine (optional)

FOR THE GARLIC HOLDER the rods used are simply tied together to seal the bottom. It has been designed to hold a few bulbs of garlic, but if you want to make a larger or wider basket you can just add more rods, but remember to always have an odd number of rods at the start. I have suggested at the end of the project that the basket be squashed together to make an oval only because if you were to hang it on a wall it will hang better that way. Leaving it round is an option if you prefer. If you can source willow long and fine enough to make a deeper basket, then it could be possible to use this design to make a wooden-spoon holder or vegetable basket.

1

2

3

STEP 1

You begin by temporarily securing 9 rods together with tape 15cm (6in) down from the tips. Find a comfortable place to sit so you can grip the rods between your knees, as you will need both hands free to weave. Above the tape, fold all the rods down to a right angle so that they splay out. In this example 1 of the rods is green to help you understand the route each rod takes. To start, take the green rod and lift it up and over to fold it across the next 2 rods.

STEP 2

Where the green rod crosses the second rod, lift that second rod over the green 1 and lay it across the next 2 rods. This

is the patten used all the way through the basket. Each time you lift 1 rod and lay it across 2 rods, you take the second rod crossed from underneath and lift it over and across the next 2 rods, and so on.

STEP 3

Keep turning the basket clockwise as you work. After 8 movements you will arrive at the place where you started. You simply carry on in the same pattern, crossing over 2, picking up the second 1 crossed and folding that 1 over the next 2, and so on.

STEP 4

Now you have got started it's worth giving a thought to the shape. Where you make the folds affects the shape of the basket. The folds can be directly on top of the fold beneath – this would make a tube – or if you fold to the side, you will begin to increase the length of your stroke and consequently the circumference of the basket. The latter technique is what is used for the Garlic Basket. It's important to try to keep the same tension on both rods when you make the twist to fold.

4

STEP 5

As the shape gets deeper, the strokes need to be longer to allow the circumference to widen. As with the other spiral projects you can stop weaving wherever you like. In the same way as for the Napkin Ring and Bird Feeder (see pages 76 and 80), to finish the basket you simply slide a rod into the row underneath. You will have a single butt in each space, but 1 space will have 2 butts.

5

STEP 6

Using the secateurs, trim the ends leaving 5mm (⅜in). Before your basket dries and becomes inflexible, you can gently squeeze it into an oval shape, which helps it to hang flat, and therefore more securely, against a wall, or you could tie a loop into the top so it can hang freely.

6

CHAPTER FOUR

ROUND WEAVE

There are many ways to create something round in willow. It is generally thought that a round object is easier to build than oval or square one. The projects in this chapter use four very different methods. Starting with the Wreath gives you a chance to understand the dialogue between you and the material while making a simple object. The Lampshade is not strictly round weaving, but achieves a tubular form in a contemporary application of willow weaving. It introduces you to wrapping willow around an existing frame, which will allow you to easily explore other round shapes and sizes as you begin to develop an understanding of how to handle this material. The Cloche and the Coracle use very traditional techniques and are archetypal forms that have been used for centuries, but here they have been redesigned to offer very contemporary functions. The Waste-paper Bin brings you on to completing a more traditional way of building a conventional form in willow. So if you haven't made a basket before, it may be wise to start with a round one.

WREATH

WHAT YOU NEED

For the weaving:
soaked or semi-green willow, 8 rods
  2m (6½ft) long

Tools:
secateurs, a bottle/wooden pole to wrap the
  weavers around for flexibility

THE WREATH IS THE SIMPLEST and quickest of the round-weave projects. For this design I have used eight rods altogether, but you could carry on wrapping in the same pattern to make a thicker wreath.

A willow wreath can be used in many ways. It offers a beautiful natural structure to which you can add many different styles of foliage for as many different occasions. Holly, ivy and mistletoe are obvious choices at Christmas time, but the wreath can be used for many other celebrations during the year. Dressing it with spring flowers and moss as a centrepiece on a table can look stunning. Or try hanging it on a wall adorned with hops and apples in the autumn – this also looks fabulous.

STEP 3

Wrap the remaining half of the rod around your hoop 4 times until the tip meets the butt. The shape will feel a little out of balance until you put the next rod in.

STEP 4

Start opposite the first butt, but insert it so it is travelling in the other direction. Notice in the picture the top butt is pointing to the right and the lower butt is pointing to the left, and both are sitting on top of the circle, with the tips underneath. It's important to get this sequence right. If you wrap your rods in the same direction the wreath wouldn't hold together as well. Wrap the rod 7 times around the hoop. On the seventh wrap you should finish with the tip at the place where the butt started.

STEP 5

Thinking of the numbers on a clock face, you have 2 butts sitting on top of your hoop at 6 and 12 o'clock. Add in another 2 butts, 1 at 3 o'clock and another at 9 o'clock, making sure the butts are inserted in opposite directions, as you did with the first 2. You should now have 4 butts on top of your wreath and 4 tips underneath. You have used 4 rod so far, and are halfway there.

STEP 6

Turn your wreath over and repeat Steps 4 and 5 so that you finish with another 4 butts on the second side. The wreath will start to become more and more solid as you wrap more into it. For this design we have used 8 rods, but you could carry on wrapping in the same pattern to make a thicker wreath. (To make a larger wreath I would advise using longer willow.) Trim all butts and tips with secateurs, leaving a short slype cut.

To decorate, you can wind twines of foliage around the wreath, as I have done here with mistletoe (see above left and page 95).

STEP 1

To start, prepare each rod by wrapping it around a bottle or large piece of cylindrical wood to encourage the fibres into shape. This helps to avoid kinks in your rods as you wrap the willow, which would be very visible in this design (see Step 6 of Fruit Basket, page 67). With a firm grip, hold the butt end very tightly against the mould as you wrap the remaining rod away from you until you reach the tip. It will spring off in a spiral and will be easier to weave. Starting with 1 willow rod, curve half of it to make a circle of 20cm (8in) diameter.

STEP 2

It may take a few goes to achieve a smooth circle without a kink, as with the first wrap with the first rod you will find there is a lot of disparity between the strength of the butt end and the part of the rod that wraps over it. Encouraging a good, generous curve at the butt end with your left hand and holding it there firmly with your thumb will help to retain a consistent circle.

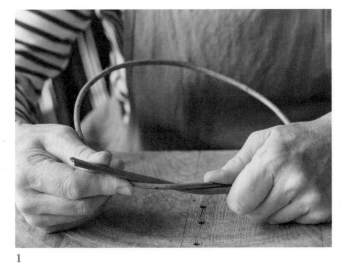

1

2

3

4

5

6

LAMPSHADE

WHAT YOU NEED

For the template:
1 lampshade bulb connector ring 20cm (8in)
    in diameter
2 plain hoops 20cm (8in) in diameter
1 plain hoops 22cm (8½in) in diameter
 – all painted to a colour of your choice if preferred

For the weaving:
soaked or semi-green willow, 80 rods 150cm
    (5ft) long (this will give you a lot to cut off, but
    anything shorter would be too thin for the size
    of the shade)

Tools:
secateurs, bodkin

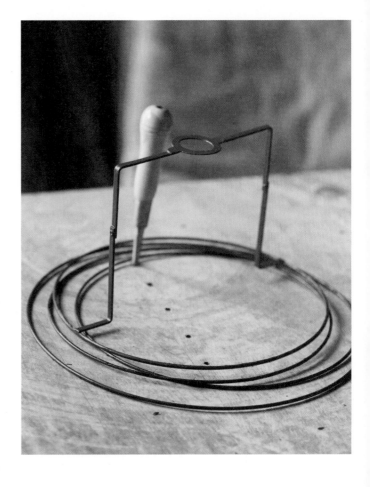

THE LAMPSHADE DOESN'T EMPLOY traditional basket-making techniques, but it does require some precise folding of material. The willow needs to be folded double around a very thin metal hoop. This is a lot to ask of a tree! So your material needs to be very good quality, soaked and mellowed to its best. If you still have trouble folding your material you could try using a pair of pliers to pinch and crush the willow fibres before you fold.

Depending on the diameter of the lampshade hoops you choose, shades can be made in the same way for different sizes, but do remember to increase the size of your willow if you increase the size of your hoop. I have used only one type of willow and hoops that are close in size, but bear in mind you could use lots of different types and colours of willow and vary the sizes of the rings.

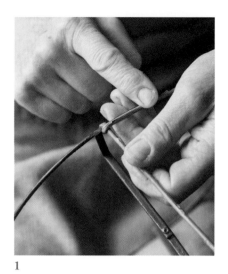
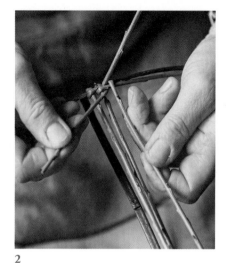

1   2   3

STEP 1

The very fine ends of the tips are too weak to make a strong connection to the lampshade frame, so start by cutting 20cm (8in) off the tip of all the rods. Hold the bulb connector ring on your lap with the bulb connector pointing towards your feet. Take the first rod and rest the tip end firmly on the hoop. Fold it very positively around the hoop, bringing the tip up to the right to then fold firmly over to the left to sit in line with the hoop.

STEP 2

When you repeat with the second rod, be sure to wrap it over the tip of the first rod as well as the hoop, placing it as close as possible to the first. Before you place the third rod, pull back the tail of the first rod up and outside of the hoop to allow you to place the third rod close to the second. When you fold the third, be sure to include the tail of the second, and so on. So, in short, every time you tie on a new rod, you leave behind a tail.

STEP 3

Continue all the way around the hoop. When you get to the last one, thread it in through from the back to the front of the first tie. You will need to use your bodkin to make a space.

STEP 4

You are now ready to add the first of the 20cm (8in) rings. Select every other stake all the way around the lampshade, then place the ring around the rods selected. If you have an odd number of

stakes you will have 2 rods running together – this is fine. Repeat to attach the second ring, but with the opposite stakes, so that the rods cross between the rings. Repeat for the third ring.

STEP 5

You need to secure the third hoop in a level position before the next stage. To do this, mark 4 of the rods that sit on the inside of the bottom ring at 3, 6, 9 and 12 o'clock, at a distance from the bulb-connector ring that is equal to the height you want for your lampshade – in this case 50cm (1½ft). Carefully fold the 4 rods from the inside to the outside of the shade directly on the marks. Gently curve the butt back underneath the second ring, allowing the butt to come back to the outside of the first hoop. This is where it lies to finish. Do this 3 more times on the marks you have made, allowing the final hoop to hang evenly and securely. Continue to fold the rest of the rods from the inside of the shade in the same way. Do this gradually, in different places around the hoop, to avoid distortion.

STEP 6

Now all the rods sitting on the outside of the third hoop have to be folded to the inside and threaded back so they sit on the outside of the second hoop. During all this folding in and out of the hoops take care not to cross any of the rods: they should lie in line with themselves. Using the secateurs, trim by cutting a very shallow slype, leaving the butts to sit against the first and second rings. Then trim the tips, leaving 1cm (½in) or so.

4

5

6

CLOCHE

WHAT YOU NEED

For the template:

1 pot 45cm (17in) in diameter, filled with soil
or sand

For the weaving:

soaked or semi-green willow,

12 thick rods 240cm (7½ft) long for the stakes

12 medium rods 210cm (6½ft) long for the
bottom wale

6 medium rods 210cm (6½ft) long for the
rising wale

12 thin rods 180cm (6ft) long for the
top wale

Tools:

secateurs, bodkin, beater

A CLOCHE CAN BE USED in many ways. I use mine mostly to support my peonies in late spring. As the plants grow the foliage finds its way through the cloche, giving the centre of the plant a strong structure to support the heavy-headed flowers. Introducing cloches to your borders gives a lovely, natural feel to your garden. Wrapped in clear plastic, cloches can also become portable greenhouses to protect early plants from frost. If you are a keen gardener you will find them an invaluable part of your tool kit.

I have specified the size of pot to make this cloche in, and the appropriate size and length of willow for that pot. You could use a different-sized pot, but remember to adjust the size of your willow accordingly. If you don't have a suitable pot to work from you can push the stakes directly into a soft piece of ground.

STEP 1

To start, push the butt end of the 12 thick rods into the pot around the circumference until they reach the bottom. To space the rods evenly, picture a clock face, and position the first 4 rods at 3, 6, 9 and 12 o'clock, then the remaining 8 rods equally spaced in between. These will be your stakes.

STEP 2

Using 12 medium rods 210cm (6½ft) long, complete a Three-rod Wale (see page 38).

2

STEP 3

Before you begin the next step, tap down the wale with the beater and check that your weaving is level. To get to the top of the cloche we are going to use a variation on the Three-rod Wale, called a rising wale. Push 3 rods 210cm (6½ft) long into the wale alongside 3 adjacent stakes. Push them in on the left-hand side of the stakes. Repeat on 3 stakes on the opposite side.

3

4

5

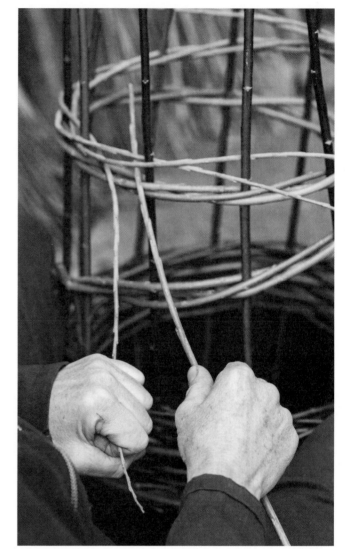

6

STEP 4

Begin either set of 3 by taking the left-hand 1 of the new additions and allow it to travel in front of 2 stakes and behind a third, allowing it to rise to a height of 10cm (4in).

STEP 5

Take the second new addition and lay it over the first, allowing it to travel in front of 2 stakes and behind a third. Repeat with the third rod, allowing each movement to increase in height. Stop working these 3 rods and repeat these movements with the opposite set of 3. Continue to work both sets of 3 using the

Three-rod Wale technique, allowing the weave to travel up the side of the basket as you go. You need to weave a few steps with 1 set, stop, then turn the basket so you can weave a few steps with the second set. This is so you don't mix up the 2 sets. You end up with 2 spirals of weaving, as in a double helix.

STEP 6

For strength its necessary to add another Three-rod Wale using 12 of the thin rods. Start in 2 places on top of the double helix with the tips. Remember to think about using the wale to control the position of your stakes to create a fluent circle.

STEP 7

Now it's time to make the lovely segmented top. First trim 20cm (8in) off the tip of each stake, making it easier to thread through the top wale. Start anywhere, threading the tip right through the wale alongside its opposite rod. You will need to use the bodkin to make a space first. Gently pull it down, retaining the natural curve, until it is 15 cm (6in) above the wale. Repeat with its pair, and then continue with the rest of the stakes. You will find that your last pair will sit much higher than the first. This is how it should be. Trim all the tips and butts from the stakes and the wales.

It's sometime difficult to get the cloche out of the pot or ground because the process of weaving fixes it so firmly in place. The easiest way to deal with this is to ease a section of it at a time by holding the bottom wale and pulling it upwards.

7

CORACLE SEAT

WHAT YOU NEED

For the template:
a soft piece of ground to work on
2 disc shapes to create the oval

For the weaving:
soaked or semi-green willow,
  18 thick rods 300cm (10ft) long for the stakes
  84 medium rods 270cm (8½ft) long for the
  7 sets of wale
  30 medium rods 150cm (5ft) long to weave
  the seat

Tools:
secateurs, loppers, basket maker's knife, bodkin,
  beater, panel pins, pin hammer

A CORACLE IS A SMALL, very strong, round boat made from willow and hazel and covered with a watertight material. It was light enough to carry some distance. Coracles were used to cross rivers to shorten the length of a journey from one village to another. Before the invention of the car, if you wanted to travel to visit a relative who lived on the other side of the river to you, you may have had to walk for miles or days to see them. People who had access to willow and hazel would weave these little one-man boats, cover then with cowhide and use them to cross the river.

I have used the concept of this construction and turned it upside down to create a robust but simple seat for two. When making a basket, one would normally work from left to right. The strength needed for the Coracle Seat is created by working the bands of Three-rod Wale in opposite directions. One set is woven from left to right, and the next set is woven from right to left. For clarity, I have woven these bands in different colours so you can follow how the sequence works. It also produces a rather nice striped, herringbone effect.

1

STEP 1

Choose a good piece of stone-free, flat ground that no one minds you poking holes in. To help you make a perfect oval shape lay down, side by side, 2 identical circles of at least 40cm (16in) diameter. I have used 2 ceramic pot trays as my template. Standing so the circles are one above the other, push 7 of the thickest rods into the ground around 1 half of an oval. If you think of a clock face as your reference, place them at 9, 10, 11, 12, 1, 2 and 3 o'clock on the top circle. Push them in to a depth of 20cm (8in) to make sure they are stable enough to weave around. Repeat from the other end. You will now have 4 thick rods left. They are used on each side to fill the gap between the 2 half circles to complete the oval.

STEP 2

You are now ready to do a Three-rod Wale (see page 38), using the medium rods 270cm (8½ft) long. When you have completed this first set use your beater to tighten and level the weave, then continue to weave a second set of wale with another 12 rods. To add in this new set start with the tips, inserting them alongside the tips from the first wale.

2

3

4

5

STEP 3

Complete the second wale with all 12 rods, ending with tips.

STEP 4

The Coracle Seat needs to be very strong as it is designed for 2 people to sit on. To achieve this, the waling technique is completed 7 times, thus using 84 rods in total. If we were to weave the wale in the same direction for all 7 layers the seat would have a tendency to twist and loose shape. To counteract this, change the direction of the next 2 layers of wale. Previously we have built a wale moving from left to right. The next 2 layers of wale need to move from right to left. Start in the same way as before and weave another 2 sets of wale, using your beater to tighten and level each set.

STEP 5

You have now woven 4 sets of wale. Set 5 and 6 are woven back in the other direction, starting with your tips on the left and working to the right. The last wale, number 7, is woven the other way again, starting with your tips on the right and working towards the left. Check that your weaving is level by using the beater to beat down any high points.

6

7

STEP 6

You are now ready to make the seat with the remaining lengths of the uprights. Place your knife 1cm (½in) above the wale to gently kink each of the stakes to a right angle over the centre of the seat (see Step 2 of Square Template, page 35). Beginning with the rods on the short sides bring down one rod at a time at each end to judge where to make the second kink to fold into the weaving opposite. Cut off the tip, leaving a slype about 6cm (2½in) long to help you cram the kinked rod into the opposite side of the wale. You may need to use the bodkin to make a space first. Once kinked use the side of the beater to tap them into place. Continue to pair up these stakes with this technique leaving 4 stakes on each of the long sides.

STEP 7

Taking the first opposite pair on the long sides, weave across the short length, crossing only once before cramming them into the other side of the wale.

STEP 8

Weave only 1 pair at a time, as you have to make a simple under-over weave in between each pair to make the seat. To do this, cut a 2cm (¾in) slype on the end of the weaver and poke it into the wale to secure it to start.

STEP 9

To weave the seat there is no firm pattern. Start by inserting the butt into the wale then weave until you get to the next pair of stakes to be folded down.

STEP 10

Continue to the other end, weaving between the paired stakes and taking them across as you go. Trim all the ends.

STEP 11

It won't be possible to pull the seat out of the ground in one go. Ease it out by going around and around, pulling a section at a time. To secure the weaving at the base, knock a panel pin directly through the weaving and into each stake. Trim the stakes level with the weave then trim the inside. Well done, this is a heavy piece to work with. Make a cup of coffee and enjoy sitting on your very own Coracle Seat.

8

9

10

11

WASTE-PAPER BIN

For the template:
Round Template (see page 36) – 20cm (8in) in
   diameter and 7.5mm (⅓in) thick at the butt,
   made from green or semi-green willow, then
   dried before use

For the weaving:
4 dry sticks 25cm (10in) long and 5mm (⅜in)
   thick at the butt for the base
soaked willow,
   22 thick rods 150cm (5ft) long for the stakes
   52 medium rods 90cm long (3ft) for 2 sets of
   randing and weaving in the base
   24 thin rods 150cm (5ft) long for the bottom
   and top wale

Tools
basket maker's bench and chair, basket maker's
   knife, secateurs, Sellotape (Scotch tape), panel
   pins, pin hammer, string or hoop, 2 bodkins,
   weight, beater, pliers

I USED THE WASTE-PAPER BIN in Key Techniques to illustrate the three most important stages of building a basket. These stages are Three-rod Wale, a Rand and a Border (see pages 38–41). However, this is the first project in the book that uses a Catalan way of building a basket, so-called because this construction originated in the Spanish region of Catalonia. The method is unique in that the stakes are first woven into the base, as opposed to attaching them to the base afterwards. This makes it very strong and there is less need for a lot of knife work, so it is very suitable for a beginner.

A waste-paper bin is a very popular item. Nearly every room in a house needs one so you can't go wrong if you make this as a gift for someone. I have used two different colours for mine, to make it easier to tell the difference between the bands of waling and randing.

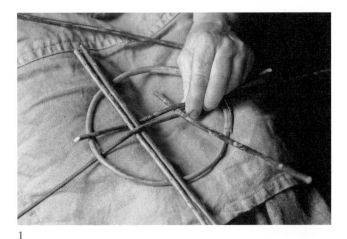

1

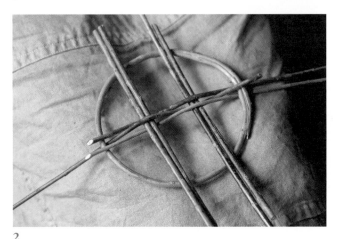

2

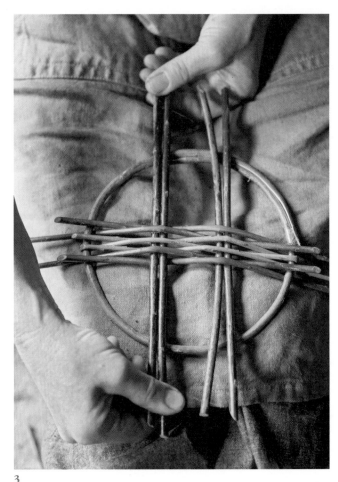

3

STEP 1

Begin the base by working with the template on your lap. Note where the template join is in relation to the weaving. Lay out 2 pairs of dry sticks, along with the 22 thickest rods for your stakes and 8 of the 52 medium rods for your weavers.

To start, take 1 stake and lay the butt end on top of the right-hand side of the template with the other end sitting underneath the left-hand side of the template. Lay the right-hand pair of dry sticks in position on top of that stake, as shown. Then take the second stake, pass it underneath the right-hand side of the template and lay it over the top of the pair of dry sticks with the butt end sitting on top of the left-hand side of the template. At this point you may wish you had a third hand! Take 1 of the second pair of dry sticks and feed it in between the 2 stakes to create a weave. Once it is secure and sitting firmly across the template, add its pair.

STEP 2

Position the 2 woven stakes so they are in the centre of the template ready for the next step of weaving. Using 1 of the 8 medium weavers, start with the butt on top of the template on the right-hand side. Weave 3 rows, folding tightly around the template, ending with the tip end on the left-hand side. Weave in 2 more stakes, making sure your butts are always on top of the template. This is now your pattern: 2 stakes, 1 weaver.

STEP 3

The dry sticks have a back and a belly. While you have been weaving the orientation of the sticks might have moved. In the photograph above you can see that 1 pair is parallel. In the other pair the curved stick needs to be turned until the back is up and the belly is down. This makes the weaving more precise. You might need to correct this a few times as you weave the base.

4

5

6

STEP 4

To finish the first half of the base and close the remaining gap, weave the last 3 rows with a medium weaver around the dry sticks only. Finish on the top or bottom of one of the pairs of dry sticks.

STEP 5

Turn the base around and repeat the same weaving pattern to complete the second half. This pattern ensures that your stakes are suitably placed for weaving the sides and making a good border. Depending on the thickness of your willow, you will have approximately 14 stakes and 8 weavers in the base.

STEP 6

Next we bring up the stakes to make the sides. If you just pull them up they will slide out of place, so you need to create some tension by putting the base onto a flat floor surface and placing your foot firmly on top before starting. Gently but firmly fold up the stakes one by one to a right angle, and hold them in place with the other hand. The idea is not to pull, but to encourage.

7

8

9

STEP 7

Using a hoop or a loop of string, place all the stakes inside to hold them so your hands are free to trim the base.

STEP 8

You will then see that you have 4 natural spaces, either side of the dry sticks at each end, that need to be filled with the remaining 8 stakes. With your secateurs, cut a short slype on the butt end of each stake and slide them into the spaces, as shown, until the ends of the opposite stakes meet inside the base weave.

STEP 9

Use the tip of your basket maker's knife to create the fold to bring up the last 8 stakes. Fold them positively to a right angle and place them inside the hoop with the others. You are now ready to start weaving the sides, but first you need to secure your basket base to the bench with a thin bodkin and a weight.

A Three-rod Wale is next. Using 12 thin rods altogether, follow the steps in Three-rod Wale (see page 38). As you weave, imagine the shape you are aiming for by paying attention to the angle of your stakes, and utilize the Three-rod Wale to create equal spaces between the stakes. Check the wale is level with your beater.

10

STEP 10

The English Rand is next. There are 2 lots of English Rand and so for clarity I have woven the first in a green willow and the second in a brown willow. You will use 22 medium weavers in the first rand and another 22 in the second. You can begin the rand anywhere. Follow all the steps in English Rand (see page 39). As you weave, the basket will begin to take on a shape of its own. It will take little practice to control this. You need to make a very clear decision about the position of the stakes as you weave around them with the rand. Put simply, if you want your basket to flare out more you would pull the stake towards you as you lay the weaver behind it. Conversely, if you want your basket to be more tubular you would push the stake inward as you weave in front of it. This will help to avoid any corrugation. This awareness of how to control the uprights also helps you to keep the stakes parallel as you weave.

Before starting the top wale check again that the weaving is level by using your beater. Add another Three-rod Wale, using the remaining 12 thin rods. On to the last stage, a Five-pair Border (see page 40). Trim all the ends inside and out, and your basket is complete.

CHAPTER FIVE

SQUARE WEAVE

Among basket makers a perfectly square basket is held in high esteem. The manufacturer who can weave all the sides to the correct length with all four corners in the right place is a deeply respected and admired crafter. The making of a square basket is considered to be the prerogative of the experienced. However, a square basket is very popular and useful. Using the Catalan way of building shortens the journey to a perfectly square basket. Firstly, there are no square corners to be made – the border simply continues in the same pattern all the way around. These are known as 'round corners'. Secondly, the position of your stakes is dictated by the pattern woven into the base, so maintaining sides of equal lengths is more achievable.

If you are a newcomer to basket making I would suggest that before you make any of the other projects in this section you have a go at the Trivet (see page 122). There are no stakes, so it is a gentle introduction to the pattern and to weaving with a heavier material. The rest of the projects have sides and so the bases have the stakes woven into them. When weaving the stakes into a base it's very important that the butts sit on the top of the template frame, because when you fold up the stakes to form the sides they need to travel up from underneath the base to form a firm side wall, and they need to be anchored firmly.

As I mentioned at the outset of the Projects section, sometimes when a basket is complete, the base no longer sits perfectly flat. This is particularly true of square weaves, so always re-set your basket before it dries out to can avoid any permanent wobble, which would be very annoying.

TRIVET

WHAT YOU NEED

For the template:
Square Template (see page 35) – 33 x 20 cm
   (12 x 8in), using 2 rods 270cm (8¹/₂ft) long and
   1cm (¹/₂in) thick at the butt, made from green or
   semi-green willow, then dried before use

For the weaving:
8 dry sticks, 50cm (1¹/₂ft) long and 7.5mm (¹/₃in)
   thick at the butt
soaked willow,
   40 thick rods 150cm (5ft) long for the weaving

Tools:
basket maker's knife, secateurs, Sellotape (Scotch
   tape), panel pins, panel hammer, thin willow ties
   or string, bodkin, pliers, beater

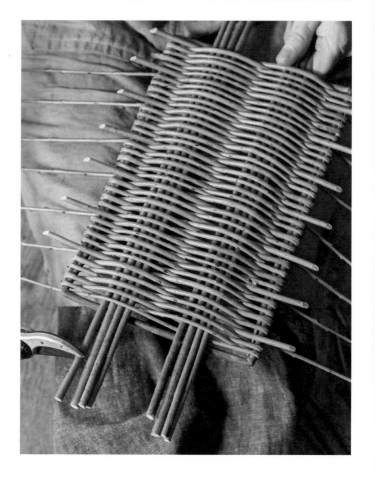

THIS SIMPLE INTRODUCTION TO SQUARE WEAVE uses the same size and shape template shown in Square Template (see page 35). The construction and weave pattern is a stepping stone to the other projects in this chapter: the Breakfast Tray, Jardinière, Lunch Bag and Laundry Basket.

   This Trivet is very useful for presenting canapés or fruit, as a centrepiece on a table and it is also very useful as a hot plate in the kitchen. Many people are surprised that willow will tolerate the intense heat from a hot dish straight from the oven but, once tested, a woven trivet becomes an invaluable kitchen tool. The handles are a useful practical addition, as well as adding to the visual appeal.

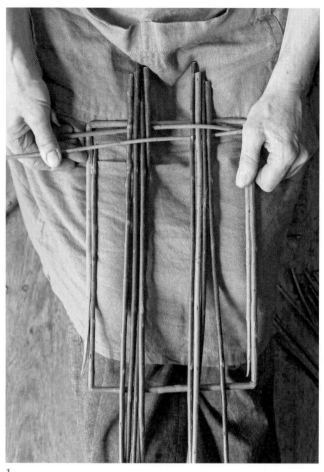

1

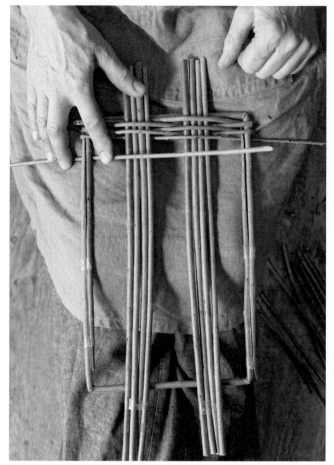

2

STEP 1

Before you start to weave, separate your dry sticks into 2 sets of 4. Holding the template on your lap, wrap your first weaver around the left-hand side of the template, using the butt of the weaver. Insert the first set of 4 sticks on the left as you begin to weave the second row, then secure the second set of sticks. It can be a bit tricky to hold until you have completed the movement. Weave out this first rod, weaving 3 or 5 rows, whichever the length allows. It's important to weave an odd number of rows to maintain the pattern.

STEP 2

Take the second weaver and thread it underneath the frame on the right. Weave the butt over the right-hand set of sticks then underneath the left-hand set of sticks so that it rests on the template on the left-hand side next to the tip of the previous weaver. Until you have woven a little way, you may find that the 2 sets of sticks won't stay parallel. I sometimes stick them altogether temporarily with some Sellotape (Scotch tape) to help control them. They also need to be positioned and woven with the belly down. It's possible to turn them to this position partway through your weaving with the pliers. This helps to give even tension.

3

STEP 3

Weave 3 or 5 rows so that the tip ends up on the right-hand side of the template, and underneath. Then start with another butt above this tip. Continue this sequence all the way to the other side. You should have all the butts sitting on the top of the template, alternating left and right. As the gap gets smaller you can bend the weaver to a right angle behind the sticks to help you get the weaver into a small space.

STEP 4

When you get to the top there may not be a space to weave a complete rod. As long as you weave 2 rows or more it will all hold together. A single row would drop out when dry. Trim all the ends close to the template, but trim the dry sticks 5cm (2in) longer so they can be used as handles.

4

BREAKFAST TRAY

WHAT YOU NEED

For the template:
Square Template (see page 35) – 42 x 28 cm
(16¹⁄₂ x 11in), using 2 rods 300cm (10ft) long and
1cm (¹⁄₂in) thick at the butt, made from green or
semi-green willow, then dried before use

For the weaving:
12 dry sticks, 55cm (21¹⁄₂in) long and 7.5mm (¹⁄₃in)
thick at the butt
soaked willow,
38 medium rods 180cm (6ft) long for the stakes
20 medium rods 150cm (5ft) long to weave the base
24 thin rods 180cm long (6ft) for the wale

Tools:
basket maker's bench and chair, basket maker's knife,
secateurs, beater, pliers, 2 bodkins, string, measure

MAKING A SHALLOW TRAY with willow can be a clumsy process. This Breakfast Tray employs just two sets of Three-rod Wale (see page 38) and a Five-pair Border (see page 40), which makes this low, square piece manageable and uncomplicated to make, but also strong in structure. With this design it would be very simple to increase the height by adding more sets of wale or introducing a rand, if you wanted to create a deeper-sided basket for storing logs, shoes or toys. If you do this, remember to increase the size of your stakes for the border, so that when you come to weave the border the rods are thick enough to make a solid rim.

Once constructed a tray has many uses. We regularly have our lunch outdoors and so use our trays not just for breakfast, but to carry food to and from the kitchen. And having a tray sitting at the bottom of the stairs to collect all sorts of sundries that have made their way down really helps to keep domestic life in order.

1

STEP 1

Before you start to weave, separate out 8 of the dry sticks into 2 sets of 4. Holding the template on your lap, lay the sticks across the template. Using 2 of your 38 stakes, position the first 1 so that the butt sits on the right-hand side of the template, travels under the first set of 4 dry sticks and over the second, ending with the rod underneath the template on the left-hand side. Do the opposite with the second stake. These are your first 2 stakes, which are now securely woven into the base. Position them as close to the bottom of the template frame as you can.

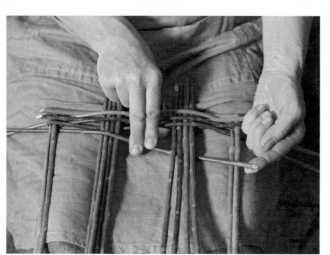

2

STEP 2

Now you need to weave a few rows before you add the next 2 stakes. Selecting from the 24 thin rods and starting with the butt of 1 in the position shown, weave 2 more rows. That's 3 altogether with this weaver, so the tip will finish on the right-hand side. Weave 3 more rows with a second weaver, starting with the butt where the last tip finished on the left-hand side.

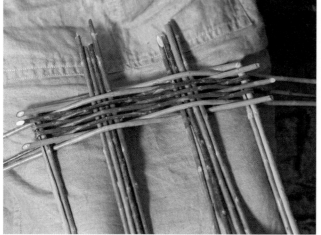

3

STEP 3

Add 2 more stakes as in Step 1. For clarity I have woven this base using green willows for the stakes and brown willows for the weavers. As you weave, keep checking that the dry sticks stay belly down.

4

STEP 4

When you have woven halfway, you need to add in 4 more dry
sticks to the base so that your 2 pairs of 4 become 2 pairs of 6.
This gives a more solid weave in the base and, more importantly,
it creates the correct spacing for inserting the stakes on the short
side later. Cut a 2cm (¾in) slype on 1 end in order to push them
through the weave. Sometimes tapping them through with the
beater is easier. Make sure they sit with the belly down, and
adjust the other sticks if necessary. Continue to weave the same
pattern for the rest of the template, making sure you end with 2
stakes, as you started. You should have all the butts sitting on the
top of the template frame and all the tips underneath.

STEP 5

Now its time to bring up all the stakes on the long sides to create
the sides of your basket – follow Step 6 of Waste-paper Bin, page
117. When you have bent all the stakes, secure them as shown
with a round template or tie them into position with string. With
your secateurs trim all the ends, including the 2 sets of dry sticks.

5

6

7

STEP 6

Cut a short slype on 1 end of each of the remaining 16 stakes and push 8 into each of the short ends through the weaving in the positions shown. You may need to use your bodkin to create a space first. Drive them in some way to make them secure.

STEP 7

Kink up these stakes as you did for the long sides. Tuck all the stakes into the hoop with the others.

STEP 8

Fix your basket to the board with a bodkin and a weight inside, then you are ready to add the first wale. Start the 2 sets of wales on the left side of the each of the long sides (see Three-rod Wale page 38). As you weave the sides of a square object you need to over-accentuate the position of the stakes by pushing them in toward the centre of the basket. Use one hand to control the stakes while the other hand selects the next weaver to be woven.

STEP 9

As you approach the corner keep paying attention to the position of the stakes as you weave. The wale continues in the same pattern, but as you lay the rods around the stakes, keep a firm idea in your mind of where the corner stakes need to be, and use the weaving to control this. Complete the wale with all 12 rods. Check the height is level with the beater. Then add another wale with another 12 rods. At this point the tray should be about 5–6cm (2–2½in) high. Checked the wale is level.

STEP 10

To start a border on a square piece, always begin on the left-hand side of a longer side so you can establish the pattern before you reach the corner. Starting at a corner would make the piece less fluent. Follow Steps 1–9 of Five-pair Border (see pages 40–1).

STEP 11

Most square work requires you to change the pattern of the weave as you travel around a corner. With this method you simply carry on with the same pattern. It will feel a little different because the spacing changes, and a little more care is needed to keep the horizontals smooth as you place them into the correct space. Before the basket dries press it out firmly on a flat surface.

8

9

10

11

JARDINIERE

WHAT YOU NEED

For the template:
Square Template (see page 35) – 50 x 18cm
(18 x 7in), using 2 rods 270cm (8½ft) long and
1cm (½in) thick at the butt, made from green or
semi-green willow, then dried before use

For the weaving:
8 dry sticks, 60cm (2ft) long and 7.5mm (⅓in)
  thick at the butt
soaked willow,
  40 thin rods 180cm (6ft) long for the stakes
  26 medium rods 90cm (3ft) long for the base
  24 medium rods 150cm (5ft) long for the bottom
  and top wales
  40 medium rods 90cm (3ft) long for the randing

Tools:
basket maker's bench and chair, basket maker's
  knife, secateurs, pliers, 2 bodkins, weight,
  beater, measure

THE JARDINIÈRE BASE IS NARROWER than the Breakfast Tray, but the sides are woven in exactly the same way, with the addition of an English Rand (see page 39) between the two wales. Seeing a flash of white, neatly trimmed butts sitting consecutively on each stake within the English Rand technique is an added bonus to the pattern. The flat side of the Jardinière shows this off very well.

I always have herbs growing on my kitchen window sill, ready to pick as needed. When you buy these lovely plants they come in rather ugly plastic pots. I have every intention of repotting them into nicer pots, but never seem to get around to it. Putting them in a jardinière instantly makes them look lusciously natural. Equally, many other small potted plants look gorgeous grouped in a willow container.

1

2

STEP 1

To weave the base for the Jardinière follow Steps 1–4 of Breakfast Tray (see pages 128–9). The Jardinière is a narrower basket, so you only need 2 pairs of 3 dry base sticks. Use 28 of the stakes to weave into the base. Use 26 medium rods 90cm (3ft) to weave between the stakes. Take care as you weave to fold around the template with the right tension. If you use too much tension you may pull the sides in, making the template narrower in the middle. Fold up the stakes – follow Step 6 of Waste-paper Bin, page 117.

STEP 2

Take the remaining 12 stakes and cut a slype on 1 end of each. Insert them as far as they can go into each of the short sides, as shown, 6 to each side. Fold up these stakes as before.

Fix the base to a table using a bodkin and a weight. Weave a round of Three-rod Wale (see page 38), using 12 medium rods 150cm (5ft) long.

3

4

STEP 3

Next, follow Steps 1–3 of English Rand (see page 39), starting
anywhere, using the 40 medium rods 90cm (3ft) long. While
weaving, pay attention to keeping the corners at a right angle.
To do this, it's best to take the corner stakes out of the hoop,
holding them so they sit in a more upright position as you weave,
otherwise you will end up with a very different shaped basket.

This should bring your basket to an approximate height of
14cm (5½in), but this will depend on how thick your weavers
are. Check the level using your beater. Continue with another
wale, using the remaining 12 medium rods 150cm (5ft) long,
and holding the stakes upright at the corners as before.

STEP 4

To finish the top, follow Steps 1–9 of Five-Pair Border (see pages
40–1), finishing at a height of around 16cm (6in). As with the
Breakfast Tray, when you make the corners simply continue
weaving the same pattern. The spacing will just feel a little
different from the sides, and you will need to pay attention
to the position of the stakes.

Trim all the ends close to the weave using secateurs. Re-set the
basket to shape while it is still damp.

LUNCH BAG

WHAT YOU NEED

For the template:

Square Template (see page 35) – 28 x 10cm
  (11 x 4in), using 2 rods 210cm (6½ft) long and
  7.5mm (⅓in) thick at the butt, made from green
  or semi-green willow, then dried before use

For the weaving:

8 dry sticks, 35cm (1ft) long and 5mm (³⁄₈in) thick
  at the butt
soaked willow,
  28 thick rods 120cm (4ft) long for the stakes
  10 thin rods 120cm (4ft) long for the base
  36 medium rods 120cm (4ft) long for the bottom
  and two top wales
  28 thin rods 120cm (4ft) long for the rand
  2 leather straps 40 x 2cm (16 x ¾in), with a hole
  punched into each end

Tools:

basket maker's bench and chair, basket maker's
  knife, secateurs, 2 bodkins, weight, beater,
  pliers, measure, hole punch, Japanese side
  cutters

THIS LUNCH BAG IS SMALL but it is extraordinarily strong. Working a shape that goes from rectangular to oval and with a decreasing circumference from bottom to top makes a small item stronger than it would otherwise be, even when it is woven out of very fine willow. Many natural materials seem to sit together easily with little effort. Leather and willow make a good partnership, so it seemed obvious to add these simple leather handles, securely incorporated into the weave.

This cute little willow bag has been designed to accommodate a hearty lunch. This shape works equally well as a handbag – you could you add a longer shoulder strap to the two shorter ends. Or size it up, starting from a larger template, to make a shopping bag.

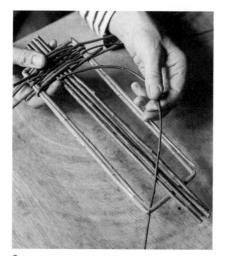

1

2

3

STEP 1

The pattern of weave in the base of this basket is slightly different from that of the other projects in this chapter in that you weave over 1 set of base sticks only. To begin, lay the 4 dry sticks on top of the template. Taking 1 of the 28 thick rods lay it over the top of the sticks and under the template on each side, with the butt on the left-hand side. Put a second one in the same place, but travelling in the opposite direction, so that the butt is sitting underneath the template on the right-hand side.

STEP 2

Now weave to fill the space before adding the next stakes. Using a thin rod and starting with the butt on top of the template on the right-hand side, weave 5 rows, ending with the tip on the opposite side of the template, on the top. Put in 2 more stakes in the same way as the first 2, but begin your next weaver with the butt on top of the template on the right-hand side. Repeat this pattern until the template is full. It's important to end with a pair of stakes. Use pliers to turn the sticks belly-side down.

STEP 3

Now insert 4 stakes on each of the short ends in the positions shown (see Step 6 of Breakfast Tray, page 130). Having brought up all of your stakes (see Step 6 of Waste-paper Bin, page 117) and trimmed all the ends on the base, peg the basket to the a board with a bodkin and weight it ready to weave the sides.

STEP 4

Follow Steps 1–4 of Three-rod Wale (see page 38), using 12 of the medium rods. Make sure the wale is level by using your beater, then you are ready to start the rand. Use 28 thin rods to weave an English Rand onto your 28 stakes (see page 39). Check the level again and add another Three-rod Wale. You are ready to attach the handles.

STEP 5

Again, check the level of the wale, then choose which stakes look suitably placed to attach both handles. Punch a hole in the leather slightly bigger than the size of the rods and slide the handle down from the tip of the rod to sit firmly onto the wale. A third wale will secure the handles, using the 12 remaining medium rods.

STEP 6

Check the level again. To finish, follow Steps 1–9 of the Five-Pair Border (see pages 40–1), This is quite a small basket, so to trim these very fine ends using the secateurs might be a little tricky. Japanese side cutters are great for this scale of work. If your basket won't sit level on a surface you can be quite forceful in pushing the form about to encourage it to sit level before it dries.

4

5

6

LAUNDRY BASKET

For the template:
Square Template (see page 35) – 34 x 34cm (1 x 1ft),
  using 2 rods 300cm (10ft) long and 1.25cm (¹/₂in) thick
  at the butt, made from green or semi-green willow,
  then dried before use

For the weaving:
12 dry sticks, 45cm (17in) long and 1cm (¹/₂in) thick at
  the butt
soaked willow,
  32 medium rods 210cm (6¹/₂ft) long for the stakes
  14 medium rods 180cm (6ft) long for the base weavers
  24 thin rods 210cm (6¹/₂ft) long for the 2 bottom wales
  64 medium rods 150cm (5ft) long for the first 2 sets
  of rand
  64 medium rods 120cm (4ft) long for the third and
  fourth sets of wale
  24 thin rods 120cm (4ft) long for the 2 top sets of wale
  2 leather straps 40 x 2cm (16 x ³/₄in), with a hole
  punched into each end

Tools:
basket maker's bench and chair, basket maker's knife,
  secateurs, beater, pliers, 2 bodkins, weight, measure,
  string or hoop, hole punch, Japanese side cutters

THIS LAUNDRY BASKET is a lovely example of weaving a shape that progresses from a square base to a round border at the top. You allow the shape to taper into a round as you weave four layers of English Rand (see page 39), grading the weaving material from thick to thin – when you get to the top the stakes are much closer together so your weavers need to be thinner and shorter. The height of this basket shows the English Rand technique at its best, with four spirals of neatly cut white butt ends. For clarity I have used different coloured willows to show the different sets of weaving. To fit a lid can be quite a task, so allowing the opening to decrease in size as you create the shape, ending up with quite a narrow gap, makes a lid unnecessary. As with the Lunch Bag (see page 136), the leather handles are a simple, natural complement.

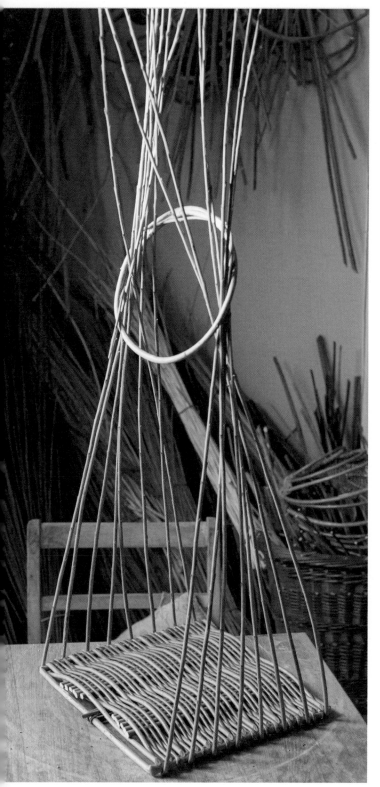

STEP 1

To make the base, follow Steps 1–4 of Breakfast Tray (see pages 128–9) using 16 of the medium rods for your stakes and 14 medium rods to weave in between. For the dry sticks you need 2 pairs of 6. Begin with only 2 in each pair, as 6 is too difficult to add all at once. Weave 5–8cm (2–3in) then add in 2 more pairs. Weave 5–8cm (2–3in) more then add in the remaining 4, so you end up with 6 in each set. Don't forget to cut a short slype on the end to slide them in. Use your pliers to twist the sticks so the bellies are facing down. Follow Step 6 of Waste-paper Bin (see page 117) to pull up all your stakes. Divide the remaining 16 stakes into 2, and insert 8 into each of the other 2 sides (see Steps 6–8 of Breakfast Tray, page 130). Kink them up with the knife and secure them in the hoop with the others.

STEP 2

Start with 2 sets of Three-rod Wale (see page 38). This will give you a very secure start. There are 4 sets of English Rand used to reach the height in this basket. Follow Steps 1–3 of English Rand (see page 39), using 32 of the medium rods 150cm (5ft) long rods. Check the level is right before going on to the next rand, using the remaining 32 medium rods 150cm (5ft) long.

STEP 3

Check the level again. Then do the third and fourth rands with the medium rods 120cm (4ft) long. Trim the ends.

STEP 4

After 4 sets of rand add the leather handles. Punch 2 holes a little larger than the diameter of the willow and thread the handle onto the willow from the tip of the rod. Wriggle it down to sit firmly on the weaving, and repeat for the other handle on the opposite side. Add another 2 sets of Three-rod Wale; a wale between the handles and border makes the basket very strong.

STEP 5

Check your levels again before adding the border. Follow Steps 1–9 of Five-pair Border (see pages 40–1). Trim all the ends on the inside and outside using secateurs or Japanese side cutters. Rebalance the basket so it sits level on the board, and leave to dry.

1

2

3

4

5

RESOURCES

There are many willow companies online, but be sure to buy from a specialist who grows willow specifically for basket making, as there are many varieties available, and not all will work for basket making. A specialist grower will have first-hand experience of the suitability of their own varieties.

Willow is usually sold dried and in bundles ranging in length from 90cm to 3.3m (3 to 11ft) tall. Rods are available in four different categories, which can be a little confusing if you are new to the world of willow – see page 19 for descriptions of these.

Jenny Crisp
Basket maker and willow grower
www.jennycrisp.co.uk
Courses are posted on my website, and some are based on the projects in this book.

The Basketmakers' Association
http://basketmakersassociation.org.uk

FOR ALL TYPES OF BASKET MAKING WILLOW:
Coates English Willow
Meare Green Court
Stoke St Gregory
Taunton TA3 6HY
www.englishwillowbaskets.co.uk

Musgrove Willows
Willow Fields
Lake Wall, Westonzoyland
Bridgwater TA7 0LP
www.musgrovewillows.co.uk

West Wales Willows
The Mill, Gwernogle
Carmathen SA32 7SA
www.westwaleswillows.co.uk

FOR WILLOW CUTTINGS ONLY:
www.jennycrisp.co.uk

FOR SPLIT CHESTNUT:
Say it with Wood
Leighton Court
Much Cowarne
Herefordshire HR8 2UN
www.sayitwithwood.co.uk

FOR TOOLS:
Knives and bodkins
www.jennycrisp.co.uk

Japanese side cutters
Mary Butcher
6 Downs Road, Canterbury
Kent CT2 7AY
www.marybutcher.net

Secateurs
www.worldoffelco.co.uk
www.vergez-blanchard.fr/boutique/liste_rayons.cfm

USA & Canada
Basket Farmer
www.basketfarmer.com/willow-sticks-for-weaving/

Bluestem Nursery
www.bluestem.ca/willows.htm

Double A Vineyards
www.doubleavineyards.com/willow-cuttings-for-sale

English Basketry Willows / Bonnie Gale
www.englishbasketrywillows.com

Plant & Gnome
www.plantandgnome.com

Vermont Willow Nursery
www.willowsvermont.com

Willow Baskets by Katherine Lewis
www.dunbargardens.com/willowcuttings

Willowglen Nursery
www.willowglennursery.com/willow.php

Australia
Nirvana Organic Farm
https://nirvanaorganicfarm.blogspot.com

ACKNOWLEDGMENTS

To Judy and David Drew for their generosity and kindness.

To Issy, Simon, Mum, Pattie and Sylvia, for their support and patience